실전 어휘 & 생활영어 200제

저자 | (주)이앤미래(대표 이동기)

공무원 영어의 시작과 끝
이동기 영어

2026
이동기 영어
실전 어휘 200제

이 책에 앞서 PREFACE

인사혁신처에서 발표한 출제 기조 전환에 따라 2025년 시험부터 공무원 영어 시험의 출제 유형이 달라졌습니다. 어휘 문제의 경우 그동안 밑줄 유의어 문제, 빈칸 완성 문제의 두 가지 유형이 출제되었고 단어뿐만 아니라 동사구나 관용 표현들도 출제되었다면 2025년 시험부터 밑줄 유의어 문제가 출제되지 않고 빈칸 완성 문제만 출제되고 있습니다. 인사혁신처는 이미 두 차례 예시 문제를 공개하여 출제 기조의 전환을 분명히 밝혔고, 2025년 국가직, 지방직 9급 시험은 그러한 출제 기조가 반영된 첫 시험이었습니다. 따라서 수험생들은 어휘의 암기만 되어 있다면 문장 전체를 읽어 볼 필요 없이 밑줄 어휘만 보고 빠르게 문제를 해결하던 기존의 문제 풀이법과는 전혀 다른 문제 풀이법이 필요합니다. 이제는 어휘 암기뿐 아니라 문장에서 빈칸을 완성할만한 단서를 찾고 논리적인 추론을 통해 빈칸에 가장 적합한 어휘를 선택하는 문제 풀이법에 대한 학습과 연습이 필요합니다. 또한 기존 출제되었던 어휘와는 범위가 다른 어휘가 출제될 것으로 예상되기에 출제 가능한 어휘의 범위를 파악해서 학습하는 선택과 집중이 무엇보다 중요합니다.

이동기 영어교육연구소는 인사혁신처의 출제 기조 전환에 대한 공지문과 두 차례 예시 문제, 2025년 기출문제의 분석뿐 아니라 이를 기반으로 유사성이 보이는 공무원 기출문제, 토익 문제, 수능 문제 등 다양한 시험들을 모두 분석하여 출제 가능한 유형과 어휘들을 정리하여 공무원 영어 기본서인 [이동기 영어 신경향 ALL IN ONE]에 수록했습니다. 또한 이런 유형분석을 기반으로 인사혁신처에서 발표한 예시 문제와 가장 유사한 문제들, 그리고 출제 가능한 문제들을 직접 출제하고 여러 차례 감수를 거쳐 이번 [이동기 영어 실전 어휘·생활영어 200제]를 출간하게 되었습니다.

[이동기 영어 실전 어휘·생활영어 200제] 이 한 권으로 새롭게 바뀌는 시험에 완벽히 대비할 수 있다고 자신합니다.

2025년 8월 연구실에서

이동기 드림

교재 활용법 GUIDE

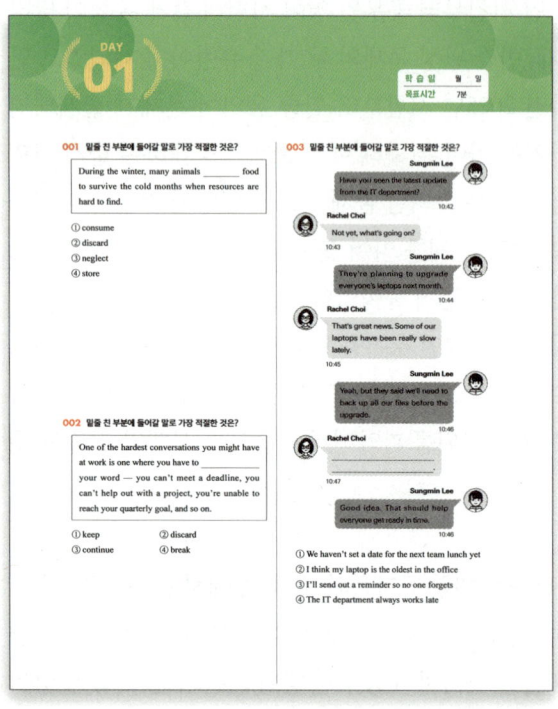

STEP 1

하루 정해진 분량(하루 10개)의 문제를 시간을 재며 먼저 풀어봅니다. 권장하는 문제 개수와 시간은 다음과 같습니다.

권장 문제 개수	10개/1일
문제당 시간	30~50초

STEP 2

각 문제의 오른쪽에 해당하는 페이지에 수록된 정답과 해설 부분을 읽고 근거를 파악해가며 꼼꼼히 학습합니다.

STEP 3

200문제를 모두 푼 후 전체 200문제 중 틀린 문제나 중요하다고 표시해 둔 문제들만 다시 꼼꼼하게 분석합니다. 내가 고른 선택지가 왜 오답인지, 그리고 정답인 선택지에 대한 근거를 정확히 찾는 등 꼼꼼한 분석이 필요합니다.

구성과 특징 STRUCTURE

1 엄선된 최빈출 어휘와 생활영어 표현
- 최근 10년간의 기출문제를 중심으로 선별된 최빈출 어휘 문제 수록
- 난이도 중~상의 실전문제 수록
- 국가직, 지방직 시험에서 적중으로 입증된 선별된 문제 수록

2 자습에 최적화된 해설과 해석
- 전 문항 꼼꼼한 해설과 해석
- 상세한 유의어와 유사 표현 정리
- 각 문제별 정답에 대한 명확한 근거 표시

3 매일 학습을 고려한 문제 구성
- 문제 구성에 있어 어휘, 표현, 생활영어 문제를 번갈아 가며 출제
- 하루 10개의 문제 풀이 권장

4 온라인을 통한 학습 지원
- 동영상 강의(gong.conects.com)를 통해 시간은 적게 들고 문제풀이 방법은 정확히 학습하는 시간 효율적인 학습
- 카페(Naver '이동기 영어')를 통한 질문과 답변, 상담

차례 CONTENTS

DAY 01	010		**DAY 11**	090
DAY 02	018		**DAY 12**	098
DAY 03	026		**DAY 13**	106
DAY 04	034		**DAY 14**	114
DAY 05	042		**DAY 15**	122
DAY 06	050		**DAY 16**	130
DAY 07	058		**DAY 17**	138
DAY 08	066		**DAY 18**	146
DAY 09	074		**DAY 19**	154
DAY 10	082		**DAY 20**	162

학습플랜 STUDY PLAN

20일 완성 학습 플랜
하루 10문제를 매일 풀어 20일을 완성합니다.

1일 완료 ☐	2일 완료 ☐	3일 완료 ☐	4일 완료 ☐
DAY 01	DAY 02	DAY 03	DAY 04

5일 완료 ☐	6일 완료 ☐	7일 완료 ☐	8일 완료 ☐
DAY 05	DAY 06	DAY 07	DAY 08

9일 완료 ☐	10일 완료 ☐	11일 완료 ☐	12일 완료 ☐
DAY 09	DAY 10	DAY 11	DAY 12

13일 완료 ☐	14일 완료 ☐	15일 완료 ☐	16일 완료 ☐
DAY 13	DAY 14	DAY 15	DAY 16

17일 완료 ☐	18일 완료 ☐	19일 완료 ☐	20일 완료 ☐
DAY 17	DAY 18	DAY 19	DAY 20

선별된
200문제로
깔끔하고 빈틈없이
정리하는
어휘·생활영어

2026 이동기 영어

실전 어휘 & 생활 영어

200제

001 밑줄 친 부분에 들어갈 말로 가장 적절한 것은?

During the winter, many animals _____ food to survive the cold months when resources are hard to find.

① consume ② discard
③ neglect ④ store

002 밑줄 친 부분에 들어갈 말로 가장 적절한 것은?

The company is trying to fill a _____ position in the marketing department because the previous manager resigned last week.

① secure ② major
③ vacant ④ distant

003 밑줄 친 부분에 들어갈 말로 가장 적절한 것은?

Sungmin Lee
Have you seen the latest update from the IT department?
10:42

Rachel Choi
Not yet, what's going on?
10:43

Sungmin Lee
They're planning to upgrade everyone's laptops next month.
10:44

Rachel Choi
That's great news. Some of our laptops have been really slow lately.
10:45

Sungmin Lee
Yeah, but they said we'll need to back up all our files before the upgrade.
10:46

Rachel Choi
_____.
10:47

Sungmin Lee
Good idea. That should help everyone get ready in time.
10:48

① We haven't set a date for the next team lunch yet
② I think my laptop is the oldest in the office
③ I'll send out a reminder so no one forgets
④ The IT department always works late

001

해석 겨울 동안, 많은 동물들은 자원을 찾기 어려운 추운 달을 살아남기 위해 음식을 저장한다.

어휘 survive 살아남다 resource 자원 consume 소비하다
discard 버리다 neglect 무시하다 store 저장하다

근거

During the winter, many animals store food to survive the cold months when resources are hard to find.

정답 ④

주요 어휘 정리
store 저장하다, 보관하다
= keep
  save
  preserve

002

해석 이전 매니저가 지난주에 사임했기 때문에 회사는 마케팅 부서의 비어있는 자리를 채우려고 하고 있다.

어휘 fill 채우다 position 자리 department 부서 previous 이전의
resign 사임하다 secure 안전한 major 주요한
vacant 빈 distant 먼

근거

The company is trying to fill a vacant position in the marketing department because the previous manager resigned last week.

정답 ③

주요 어휘 정리
major 주요한   vacant 텅 빈
= prime   = empty
  critical
  principal
  crucial
  paramount   distant 먼
  vital   = far
  momentous

003

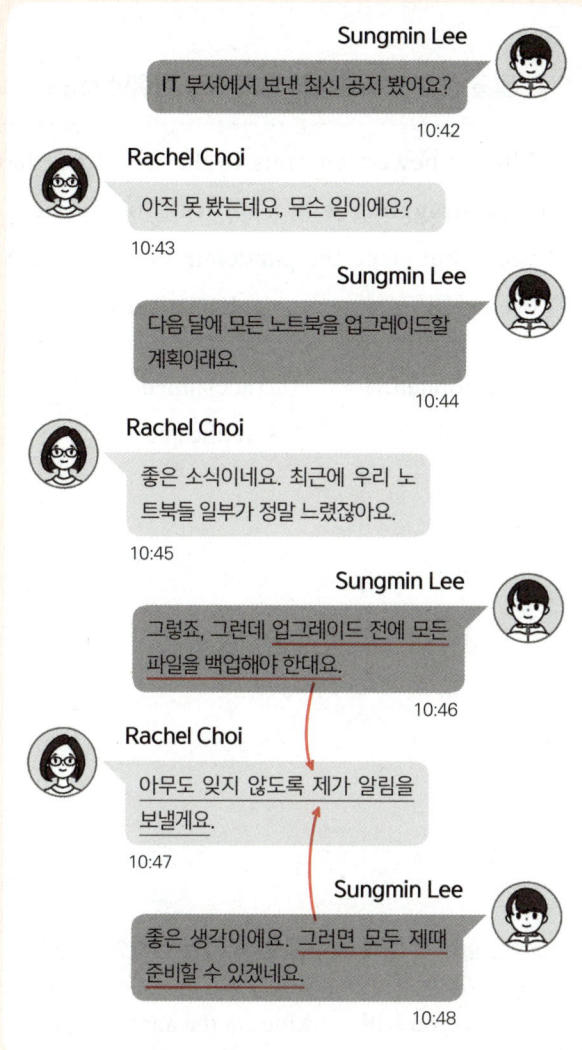

① 다음 팀 점심 날짜는 아직 정하지 않았어요
② 내 노트북이 사무실에서 제일 오래된 것 같아요
④ IT 부서는 항상 늦게까지 일하더라구요

어휘 late 최신의 laptop 노트북 컴퓨터 lately 최근에

정답 ③

DAY 01 11

004 밑줄 친 부분에 들어갈 말로 가장 적절한 것은?

> China's newest entrants to the workforce have been struggling with a difficult job market for years, but since the pandemic the situation has even _____ dramatically.

① deteriorated ② acclaimed
③ rebelled ④ replicated

005 밑줄 친 부분에 들어갈 말로 가장 적절한 것은?

> A: Are you still working on the annual report?
> B: Yes, I'm almost done.
> A: Good. The deadline is next Tuesday, right?
> B: Yes, but I might submit it tomorrow.
> A: That's early.
> B: I just want to finish it and not worry about it anymore.
> A: Oh, _____
> B: Yeah, I might plan something fun for the weekend.

① the deadline has been postponed.
② then you can relax over the weekend.
③ will you work even on the next Tuesday?
④ can you give up your weekend plan?

006 밑줄 친 부분에 들어갈 말로 가장 적절한 것은?

Ava Kim
Do you have any plans for this weekend?
10:42

Liam Park
I might go hiking if the weather's good.
10:43

Ava Kim
That sounds fun. _____
_____?
10:44

Liam Park
I'm thinking about that scenic route we talked about last month.
10:45

Ava Kim
Awesome! Can I come with you? I will bring my camera. I would like to capture the views.
10:46

Liam Park
Absolutely! The more, the merrier.
10:48

① Is there any special event you could engage in
② How often do you go hiking
③ What is the most important thing in a hiking trip
④ Have you decided on a trail

004

해석 중국의 노동인구 신규 진입자들은 어려운 고용 시장으로 수년 동안 허덕이고 있지만, 팬데믹 이후 상황은 심지어 급격히 악화되었다.

어휘 entrant 진입자 workforce 노동인구 dramatically 급격히
deteriorate 악화되다 acclaim 칭송하다 rebel 저항하다
replicate 복제하다

근거

China's newest entrants to the workforce have been struggling with a difficult job market for years, but since the pandemic the situation has even deteriorated dramatically.

정답 ①

주요 어휘 정리

deteriorate 악화되다, 나빠지다
= worsen
  degenerate

rebel 저항하다, 반대하다
= oppose
  resist
  defy
  disobey

005

A: 아직 연례 보고서 작업 중이야?
B: 응, 거의 끝났어.
A: 잘 됐다. 마감일은 다음 주 화요일이지?
B: 응, 그런데 아마 내일 제출할지도 몰라.
A: 일찍 끝내네.
B: 그냥 끝내버리고 더는 걱정하고 싶지 않아.
A: 오, 그러면 주말에 쉬겠네.
B: 응, 주말에 재밌는 계획을 세울까 해.

① 마감일이 연기되었어.
③ 다음 화요일에도 일할 거야?
④ 네 주말 계획을 포기할 수 있어?

어휘 annual 연례의 deadline 마감일 submit 제출하다
postpone 연기하다 relax 쉬다 give up 포기하다

정답 ②

006

① 네가 참여할 만한 어떤 특별한 행사가 있어
② 얼마나 자주 등산을 가니
③ 등산에서 가장 중요한 점이 무엇이니

어휘 scenic 경치가 좋은 route 경로 capture (사진을) 찍다
engage in ~에 참여하다 trail 코스

정답 ④

DAY 01

007 밑줄 친 부분에 들어갈 말로 가장 적절한 것은?

> A: I am here to get my prescription filled.
> B: Your prescription will be ready in twenty minutes.
> A: Do you ever deliver prescriptions by mail?
> B: Yes, in fact, you can renew the prescription over the Internet and have it delivered to your home.
> A: How should I take this medication?
> B; You should take it twice a day.
> A: Can I take it with food?
> B: You should take this medicine with food and no alcohol.
> A: _____?
> B: Sometimes you might feel dizzy, but that isn't common.

① Should I expect any side effects
② How often should I take this medicine
③ May I renew my prescription in advance
④ What if I forget to take my medicine

008 밑줄 친 부분에 들어갈 말로 가장 적절한 것은?

> Because working-class people tend to have lower incomes and thus they don't see any particular way to soften the impact of rising prices, they just _____ when inflation remains high.

① prosper   ② endure
③ change   ④ perish

007

A: 처방 약을 받으러 왔어요.
B: 20분 안에 처방 약이 준비될 거예요.
A: 혹시 우편으로 처방 약을 배달해주시나요?
B: 네, 사실 처방전을 인터넷으로 갱신해서 약을 집으로 배송하실 수 있습니다.
A: 이 약은 어떻게 복용해야 하나요?
B: 하루에 두 번 드셔야 합니다.
A: 음식이랑 같이 먹어도 되나요?
B: 이 약은 음식과 함께 드셔야 하고 술은 드시면 안 됩니다.
A: 부작용이 있을 수도 있나요?
B: 가끔 어지러울 때도 있지만, 그런 경우는 흔하지 않아요.

② 이 약을 얼마나 자주 복용해야 하나요
③ 미리 처방전을 갱신해도 될까요
④ 약 먹는 것을 잊으면 어떻게 하죠

어휘 prescription 처방약, 처방전　renew 갱신하다　medication 약
dizzy 어지러운　common 흔한　side effect 부작용
medicine 약　in advance 미리

정답 ①

008

해석 노동자 계층의 사람들은 소득이 더 낮은 경향이 있고 따라서 물가 상승의 영향을 완화할 어떤 특별한 방법도 보이지 않기 때문에, 인플레이션이 높은 상태일 때 그들은 그냥 견딘다.

어휘 soften 완화시키다　impact 영향　prosper 번영하다
endure 견디다　change 바꾸다　perish 소멸되다

근거

> Because working-class people tend to have lower incomes and thus they don't see any particular way to soften the impact of rising prices, they just endure when inflation remains high.

정답 ②

주요 어휘 정리
endure 견디다
= withstand
  tolerate
  bear

009 밑줄 친 부분에 들어갈 말로 가장 적절한 것은?

> Despite repeated requests, the company decided to _____ the application, stating that it did not meet the necessary requirements.

① prolong   ② approve
③ refuse   ④ review

010 밑줄 친 부분에 들어갈 말로 가장 적절한 것은?

> A: Hello, can I get a copy of my resident registration?
> B: Hi, no problem! Do you have your resident ID card with you?
> A: Oh, my gosh! I must have left it at home.
> B: Do you have _____?
> A: Let me see. Thanks god! I've brought my driver's license.
> B: That works. Just wait for a second or two. It won't take long.

① your driver's license with you when driving a car
② anything with your photo issued by the government
③ knowledge in dealing with this situation
④ time to read the guidelines in advance

009

해석 반복적인 요청에도 불구하고, 회사는 신청서가 필요한 요건을 충족하지 못했다고 말하면서 이를 거절하기로 결정했다.

어휘 application 신청서 state 말하다 requirement 요건
prolong 연장하다 approve 승인하다 refuse 거부하다
review 검토하다

근거

> Despite repeated requests, the company decided to refuse the application, stating that it did not meet the necessary requirements.

정답 ③

주요 어휘 정리
refuse 거부하다, 거절하다
= reject
  decline

010

> A: 안녕하세요, 주민등록등본을 뗄 수 있을까요?
> B: 안녕하세요, 물론이죠! 주민등록증을 가지고 오셨나요?
> A: 오, 맙소사! 집에 두고 왔나 봐요.
> B: 정부에서 발행한 사진이 붙은 어떤 것이든 가지고 있나요?
> A: 잠시만요. 다행이다! 제 운전면허증을 가지고 왔네요.
> B: 그거면 됩니다. 아주 잠시만 기다려주세요. 오래 걸리지 않을 거예요.

① 차를 운전할 때 운전면허증을
③ 이런 상황을 다루는 지식을
④ 미리 지침을 읽어볼 시간을

어휘 copy of resident registration 주민등록등본
resident ID card 주민등록증 issue 발행하다
deal with ~을 다루다 guideline 지침

정답 ②

DAY 01 17

011 밑줄 친 부분에 들어갈 말로 가장 적절한 것은?

 Guest
Hi, I have a reservation for next Saturday. I just want to confirm my booking.
10:42

 Staff
Hello! May I have your name and booking number, please?
10:43

 Guest
Sure. My name is Daniel Kim, and the booking number is BK20357.
10:44

 Staff
Thank you, Mr. Kim. Yes, your reservation for a double room on April 27th is confirmed.
10:45

 Guest
_____?
10:46

 Staff
Yes, it's part of your stay. You can enjoy it between 7:00 a.m. and 10:00 a.m. at the restaurant on the first floor.
10:47

① Is there a swimming pool at the hotel
② Can I cancel the reservation without a fee
③ Is breakfast included in my reservation
④ Do you offer a free shuttle service to the airport

012 밑줄 친 부분에 들어갈 말로 가장 적절한 것은?

A: Hello, I'd like to cancel one of the tickets I booked for the concert next week.
B: No problem. Could you give me your booking number and the name on the reservation?
A: Sure. The booking number is CX45912, and the name is Daniel Green.
B: Thank you. The refund is possible, but there's a 10% cancellation fee.
A: _____?
B: The refund will be processed to the original payment method within 5 business days.
A: That's fine. Please proceed with the cancellation.
B: Okay, I've submitted the request. You'll get a confirmation email soon.

① How long will the refund take
② Can I get a full refund
③ Why is the fee so high
④ What documents do I need to submit

013 밑줄 친 부분에 들어갈 말로 가장 적절한 것은?

Negotiations between the sides are still underway, but industry observers believe an agreement is _____.

① imminent   ② principal
③ solitary   ④ innate

011

① 호텔에 수영장이 있나요
② 비용 없이 예약을 취소할 수 있나요
④ 공항까지 무료 교통편을 제공하나요

어휘 reservation 예약 confirm 확인하다 swimming pool 수영장 cancel 취소하다

정답 ③

012

> A: 안녕하세요. 다음 주에 있는 콘서트를 예약한 표를 취소하고 싶습니다.
> B: 문제 없습니다. 예약 번호와 예약하신 이름을 알려주세요.
> A: 그러죠. 예약 번호는 CX45912이고 이름은 Daniel Green입니다.
> B: 고맙습니다. 환불은 가능하지만 10페센트의 해약금이 있습니다.
> A: 환불까지는 얼마나 걸리죠?
> B: 환불은 원래의 지불 방법으로 영업일 기준 5일 이내에 처리될 것입니다.
> A: 좋습니다. 취소 건을 진행해 주세요.
> B: 알겠습니다. 요청을 제출하겠습니다. 곧 확인 이메일을 받으실 겁니다.

② 전체 환불을 받을 수 있나요
③ 수수료가 왜 이렇게 높죠
④ 어떤 서류를 제출하나요

어휘 cancel 취소하다 book 예매하다 reservation 예약 refund 환불 cancellation fee 해약금 proceed 진행하다 submit 제출하다 confirmation 확인

정답 ①

013

해석 양측 간의 협상은 아직 진행 중이지만, 업계 참관인들은 합의가 임박한 것으로 믿고 있다.

어휘 negotiation 협상 underway 진행 중인 industry 업계 observer 참관인 agreement 합의 imminent 임박한 principal 주된 solitary 혼자 하는 innate 타고난

근거

> Negotiations between the sides are still underway, but industry observers believe an agreement is imminent.

정답 ①

주요 어휘 정리

imminent 임박한	innate 타고난
= urgent	= inborn
emergent	inherent
pressing	hereditary
imperative	natural
impending	

DAY 02

014 밑줄 친 부분에 들어갈 말로 가장 적절한 것은?

> The company's expenditure has consistently _____ its revenues because of outdated working practices resulting in high labour costs, as well as aged equipment resulting in high operational costs.

① enhanced   ② exposed
③ surpassed ④ fabricated

015 밑줄 친 부분에 들어갈 말로 가장 적절한 것은?

Ethan Reynolds
Hey, did you book the hotel yet?
10:42

 Rachel Reynolds
I was just about to, but prices are unusually high from the 12th to the 15th.
10:43

Ethan Reynolds
Really? That's off-season, isn't it?
10:44

 Rachel Reynolds
I thought the same, but apparently there's a big tech conference in the city.
10:45

Ethan Reynolds
Ah, that explains it. Should we shift our trip to the following week instead?
10:46

 Rachel Reynolds
_____
_____.
10:47

Ethan Reynolds
That works. That should save us a lot.
10:48

 Rachel Reynolds
I'll recheck the hotel availability and let you know shortly.
10:49

① Changing the dates might actually be more expensive
② That weekend is already booked for another event
③ Hotels seem to have more reasonable rates from the 19th to the 22nd
④ Moving it to the 12th to the 15th looks much cheaper

014

해석 높은 운영비를 초래하는 노후된 장비뿐만 아니라, 높은 인건비를 초래하는 구식의 업무 관행 때문에 회사의 지출은 지속적으로 수입을 초과해 왔다.

어휘 expenditure 지출 consistently 지속적으로 revenue 수입
outdated 구식의 practice 관행 result in ~을 초래하다
aged 노후된 operational 운영의 enhance 높이다
expose 노출시키다 surpass 초과하다 fabricate 조작하다

근거
> The company's expenditure has consistently surpassed its revenues because of outdated working practices resulting in high labour costs, as well as aged equipment resulting in high operational costs.

정답 ③

주요 어휘 정리

surpass 초과하다, 넘다   fabricate 조작하다, 위조하다
= exceed   = forge
  excel   falsify
  transcend   feign
  outdo   counterfeit
  outweigh

015

 Ethan Reynolds
저기, 호텔 예약했어?
10:42

Rachel Reynolds
막 하려던 참이었는데, 12일부터 15일까지 가격이 평소보다 이례적으로 비싸.
10:43

 Ethan Reynolds
정말? 그 시기는 비수기잖아, 그렇지?
10:44

Rachel Reynolds
나도 그렇게 생각했는데, 도시에 기술 대기업 컨퍼런스가 있다나 봐.
10:45

Ethan Reynolds
아, 그래서 그렇구나. 그럼 다음 주로 여행을 변경할까?
10:46

Rachel Reynolds
19일부터 22일까지는 호텔 요금이 더 합리적인 것 같아.
10:47

Ethan Reynolds
좋아. 그러면 비용을 꽤 아낄 수 있겠네.
10:48

Rachel Reynolds
호텔 예약 가능 여부 다시 확인하고 곧 알려줄게.
10:49

① 날짜를 바꾸면 사실 더 비쌀 수도 있어
② 그 주말은 이미 다른 일정이 잡혀 있어
④ 12일부터 15일로 옮기는 게 훨씬 저렴해 보여

어휘 book 예약하다 be about to 막 ~하려고 하다
unusually 이례적으로 off-season 비수기인
apparently ~했다나 봐 shift 변경하다 recheck 다시 확인하다
availability 가능 여부 shortly 곧 actually 사실
reasonable 합리적인 rate 요금

정답 ③

016 밑줄 친 부분에 들어갈 말로 가장 적절한 것은?

> Among his numberless works, not a single one was appreciated as a masterpiece though he had been consistently _____ in writing novels and poems.

① fruitless
② vague
③ prolific
④ obvious

017 밑줄 친 부분에 들어갈 말로 가장 적절한 것은?

Michelle Lee
Hello, I'm having trouble with my recent order. The item arrived damaged.
10:42

Customer Service
Sorry, could you please provide me with your order number and a photo of the damaged item?
10:43

Michelle Lee
Sure, my order number is #12345. I've attached a photo of the item.
10:44

Customer Service
Thank you for the information. We'll review the photo and process a replacement or refund for you.
10:45

Michelle Lee
_____?
10:46

Customer Service
The duration depends on the item and the nature of the issue. We'll let you know after reviewing the details.
10:47

Michelle Lee
Great, thank you for your help.
10:48

① How long will this process take
② Can I exchange it for a different color
③ Would you like me to submit anything else
④ Are those sold again as refurbished products

016

[해석] 비록 그는 소설과 시 창작에서 꾸준히 다작해왔지만 그의 무수히 많은 작품 중에서, 단 하나도 걸작으로 인정받지 못했다.

[어휘] numberless 무수히 많은　appreciate 인정하다
masterpiece 걸작　consistently 꾸준히　novel 소설　poem 시
fruitless 성과 없는　vague 모호한　prolific 다작의
obvious 확실한

[근거]

> Among his numberless works, not a single one was appreciated as a masterpiece though he had been consistently prolific in writing novels and poems.

[정답] ③

[주요 어휘 정리]

fruitless 성과 없는, 불모의　↔　prolific 다작의, 다산의, 비옥한
= unproductive　　　　　　= productive
　infertile　　　　　　　　　fertile
　unfruitful　　　　　　　　fruitful

vague 모호한　↔　obvious 분명한
= ambiguous　　= apparent
　indistinct　　　　distinct
　uncertain　　　　certain
　obscure

017

② 다른 색으로 바꿀 수 있을까요
③ 추가로 제출할 게 있을까요
④ 그런 것들은 리퍼브 상품으로 다시 팔리나요

[어휘] recent 최근의　damaged 파손된　attach 첨부하다
process 처리하다; 과정　replacement 교환　refund 환불
duration 기간　exchange 교환하다　submit 제출하다
refurbished product 리퍼브 상품: 결함이 있었던 제품을 수리해 다시 판매하는 제품

[정답] ①

018 밑줄 친 부분에 들어갈 말로 가장 적절한 것은?

> The pianist received a standing ovation because she delivered an _____ performance that moved the entire audience to tears.

① mediocre
② predictable
③ clumsy
④ extraordinary

019 밑줄 친 부분에 들어갈 말로 가장 적절한 것은?

> Many species are struggling to adapt to the rapidly _____ environment, often facing unpredictable changes in temperature, resources, and living conditions.

① fluctuating
② enduring
③ conserving
④ controlling

020 밑줄 친 부분에 들어갈 말로 가장 적절한 것은?

> A: What's on your mind?
> B: Oh. I've been thinking about our upcoming presentation.
> A: Is something bothering you about it?
> B: Well, I feel like we could add more visuals to make it more engaging.
> A: That's a good point. Do you have any ideas?
> B: _____
> A: That sounds great! By doing so, we can convey complex ideas and make them easier to remember.

① How about using charts?
② Why don't we discuss it later?
③ We are gathering stacks of ideas.
④ Don't be misled by striking visuals.

018

[해석] 그 피아니스트는 모든 관객을 감동시켜 눈물짓게 한 놀라운 연주를 했기 때문에 기립박수를 받았다.

[어휘] standing ovation 기립박수   deliver (연설·공연을) 하다
mediocre 평범한   predictable 예측할 수 있는   clumsy 어설픈
extraordinary 놀라운

[근거]

> The pianist received a standing ovation because she delivered an extraordinary performance that moved the entire audience to tears.

[정답] ④

[주요 어휘 정리]
extraordinary 비범한, 기이한 ↔ ordinary 보통의, 평범한
= exceptional   = usual
  remarkable   normal
  outstanding   common

019

[해석] 많은 종들이 빠르게 변화하는 환경에 적응하려 애쓰고 있으며, 예측할 수 없는 온도, 자원, 생활 조건의 변화를 종종 마주하고 있다.

[어휘] species 종   adapt 적응하다   rapidly 빠르게
unpredictable 예측할 수 없는   resource 자원
fluctuate 변화하다   endure 지속하다   conserve 보존하다
control 통제하다

[근거]

> Many species are struggling to adapt to the rapidly fluctuating environment, often facing unpredictable changes in temperature, resources, and living conditions.

[정답] ①

[주요 어휘 정리]
fluctuate 변동하다, 오르내리다
= vary
  change
  swing
  mutate

020

> A: 무슨 걱정 있어요?
> B: 아, 곧 있을 발표에 대해 생각하고 있었어요.
> A: 그것에 대해 무엇이 신경 쓰이세요?
> B: 음, 그걸 더 매력적으로 만들기 위해서 우리가 더 많은 시각 자료를 추가할 수 있을 것 같아서요.
> A: 좋은 지적이네요. 아이디어 있으세요?
> B: 도표를 사용하는 게 어때요?
> A: 좋은 것 같아요! 그렇게 하면, 복잡한 생각을 전달하고 그것들을 기억하기 쉽게 할 수 있겠네요.

② 나중에 의논하는 게 어때요?
③ 우리는 많은 생각들을 모으고 있어요.
④ 인상적인 시각 자료에 현혹되지 마세요.

[어휘] What's on your mind? 무슨 걱정 있어요?
upcoming 곧 있을   presentation 발표   bother 신경 쓰이게 하다
visual 시각 자료   engaging 매력적인   point 지적
convey 전달하다   complex 복잡한   chart 도표
gather 모으다   stacks of 많은   mislead 현혹시키다
striking 인상적인

[정답] ①

021 밑줄 친 부분에 들어갈 말로 가장 적절한 것은?

Robert Johnson
Shara, will you update me on the status of the client presentation at a today's meeting?
10:42

Shara Newton
Sure, I will. Actually we're about 80% done.
10:43

Robert Johnson
Is it possible that there might be any delays or difficulties?
10:44

Shara Newton
No. Everything is going according to plan. We should be able to meet the deadline.
10:45

Robert Johnson
Great to hear. Just for the sake of caution, _____
10:46

Shara Newton
Oh, my gosh! I've almost forgotten that. He is a very good client but so forgetful.
10:47

① do you think the client presentation will be successful?
② you should check if the client remembers the date.
③ do you know the final review is scheduled for today?
④ I have finalized the budget for the next client presentation.

022 밑줄 친 부분에 들어갈 말로 가장 적절한 것은?

The proposal was considered highly _____ as it was based on data-driven analysis and clear logical reasoning.

① unreasonable   ② subjective
③ rational   ④ impulsive

021

Robert Johnson 10:42
Shara 씨, 오늘 회의에서 고객 프레젠테이션 상황을 업데이트 해주시겠어요?

Shara Newton 10:43
물론이죠, 그렇게 하겠습니다. 사실 약 80퍼센트 완료되었어요.

Robert Johnson 10:44
어떤 지연이나 어려움이 있을 까요?

Shara Newton 10:45
아니오. 모든 것이 계획대로 진행되고 있어요. 마감 기한을 지킬 수 있을 거예요.

Robert Johnson 10:46
좋은 소식이네요. 단지 노파심에서 그러는데요, 고객이 날짜를 기억하는지 확인하는 게 좋겠어요.

Shara Newton 10:47
오, 세상에! 하마터면 그걸 잊어버릴 뻔했어요. 그분은 아주 좋은 고객이지만 건망증이 있거든요.

① 고객 프레젠테이션이 성공할 거라고 생각하나요?
③ 최종 검토가 오늘 예정된 걸 아시나요?
④ 다음 고객 프레젠테이션 예산을 확정했어요.

[어휘] status 상황 delay 지연 meet the deadline 마감 기한을 지키다 for the sake of caution 노파심에서 forgetful 건망증이 있는 finalize 확정하다 budget 예산

[정답] ②

022

[해석] 그 제안서는 데이터 기반 분석과 명확한 논리적 추론을 기반으로 하고 있어서 매우 합리적이라고 여겨졌다.

[어휘] proposal 제안서 analysis 분석 reasoning 추론 unreasonable 불합리한 subjective 주관적인 rational 합리적인 impulsive 충동적인

[근거]
> The proposal was considered highly rational as it was based on data-driven analysis and clear logical reasoning.

[정답] ③

[주요 어휘 정리]
rational 이성적인, 합리적인 ↔ irrational 비이성적인
= reasonable
  sensible

023 밑줄 친 부분에 들어갈 말로 가장 적절한 것은?

A doctor who _____ confidential information about patients is not behaving professionally. Doctors have to protect patients' personal information from improper disclosure.

① reveals
② conceals
③ reflects
④ alters

024 밑줄 친 부분에 들어갈 말로 가장 적절한 것은?

Dorothy Parker
Hey, have you tried the new coffee shop on Main Street?
10:42

Jim Anderson
Yeah, I stopped by yesterday. It was cozy and the espresso was amazing!
10:43

Dorothy Parker
Nice! I've been meaning to check it out. What else did they have?
10:44

Jim Anderson
They also had a large selection of baked goods. But honestly, _____.
10:45

Dorothy Parker
Really? That's disappointing. I might pass on it. No point going if the snacks aren't worth it.
10:46

① I was disappointed with their espresso
② they didn't taste that great
③ the bagels were best
④ it was considered a decent cafe

023

해석 환자에 대한 기밀 정보를 누설하는 의사는 전문가답게 행동하는 것이 아니다. 의사들은 환자의 개인 정보를 부적절한 공개로부터 보호해야 한다.

어휘 confidential 기밀의 patient 환자
personal information 개인 정보 improper 부적절한
disclosure 공개 reveal 누설하다 conceal 감추다
reflect 반영하다 alter 변경하다

근거

> A doctor who reveals confidential information about patients is not behaving professionally. Doctors have to protect patients' personal information from improper disclosure.

정답 ①

주요 어휘 정리

reveal 누설하다, 드러내다	alter 바꾸다
= disclose	= change
debunk	adjust
divulge	amend
unveil	modify
uncover	revise
unearth	rectify
let on	

024

① 에스프레소에 실망했어
③ 베이글은 최고였어
④ 괜찮은 카페로 여겨졌어

어휘 stop by 잠깐 들르다 cozy 아늑한 amazing 훌륭한
mean to ~하려 하다 a selection of 다양한
baked goods 제과류 disappointing 실망스러운
decent 괜찮은

정답 ②

DAY 03 29

025 밑줄 친 부분에 들어갈 말로 가장 적절한 것은?

A: You're soaked in rain. What happened to you?
B: I'm locked out of my apartment.
A: Where did you lose your keys?
B: I think I left them at my job. How could I forget the keys to my own apartment?
A: There is no use in feeling bad about it now. There's nothing you can do about it.
B: You're right. _____
A: Let me go look in my closet. I'll be back in a second.

① Can I stay at your place for a night?
② I should go back at work and find my keys.
③ Do you have some dry clothes I can change into?
④ May I have a glass of hot water?

026 밑줄 친 부분에 들어갈 말로 가장 적절한 것은?

French fries and soda might be delicious, but too much of these foods can leave you feeling achy and tired, and can even _____ your health.

① maintain   ② improve
③ diagnose   ④ worsen

027 밑줄 친 부분에 들어갈 말로 가장 적절한 것은?

A: Hey, I won't be able to make it to the meeting by 3 PM. Would you mind if we rescheduled?
B: No problem at all. What time works better for you?
A: How about 6 PM instead?
B: That works. I'll update the calendar invite.
A: Great, _____.
B: You're mistaken. It's an in-person meeting at the office.

① I'll join the Zoom call then
② I'll send you the meeting notes afterward
③ I'll grab dinner and see you at Room 6
④ I'll just work from home and catch up tomorrow

025

A: 너 비에 흠뻑 젖었구나. 무슨 일이야?
B: 열쇠가 없어서 아파트에 못 들어갔어.
A: 열쇠를 어디서 잃어버렸어?
B: 내 생각에는 회사에 두고 온 것 같아. 어떻게 아파트 열쇠를 잊어버릴 수가 있지?
A: 지금 그것에 대해 기분 나빠해도 소용없어. 네가 할 수 있는 일이 없잖아.
B: 네 말이 맞아. 내가 갈아입을 수 있는 마른 옷이 있을까?
A: 옷장을 한 번 볼게. 금방 돌아올게.

① 너의 집에서 하룻밤 신세 질 수 있을까?
② 직장에 돌아가서 열쇠를 찾아야겠어.
④ 따뜻한 물 한 잔 마실 수 있을까?

[어휘] soaked 흠뻑 젖은 lock out of 열쇠가 없어서 ~에 못 들어가다
there is no use in ~해도 소용없다
change into ~으로 갈아입다

[정답] ③

026

[해석] 감자튀김과 탄산음료는 맛이 있을지는 모르지만, 너무 많은 이런 음식은 당신을 아프고 피곤하게 할 수 있고, 심지어 당신의 건강을 악화시킬 수 있다.

[어휘] achy 아픈 tired 피곤한 maintain 유지하다 improve 개선하다
diagnose 진단하다 worsen 악화시키다

[근거]

French fries and soda might be delicious, but too much of these foods can leave you feeling achy and tired, and can even worsen your health.

[정답] ④

[주요 어휘 정리]
improve 개선하다   worsen 악화시키다 / 악화되다
= ameliorate   = aggravate   = deteriorate
                            exacerbate   degenerate

027

A: 저기, 오후 3시까지 회의에 못 갈 것 같아. 일정 다시 잡아도 괜찮을까?
B: 전혀 문제없어. 어떤 시간이 더 괜찮아?
A: 오후 6시는 어때?
B: 좋아. 캘린더 초대를 업데이트할게.
A: 좋아, 그럼 줌 회의에 참여할게.
B: 잘못 알고 있어. 그거 사무실에서 하는 대면 회의야.

② 나중에 회의록을 보낼게
③ 저녁 먹고 6번 회의실에서 보자
④ 그냥 재택근무하면서 내일 따라잡을게

[어휘] make it to ~에 가다 reschedule 일정을 다시 잡다
That works. 좋아. in-person 대면의 Zoom call 줌 회의
meeting note 회의록 afterward 나중에 grab (간단히) 먹다
catch up 따라잡다

[정답] ①

028 밑줄 친 부분에 들어갈 말로 가장 적절한 것은?

> She experienced extreme _____ after working long hours without a break.

① obesity   ② vitality
③ fatigue   ④ nutrition

029 밑줄 친 부분에 들어갈 말로 가장 적절한 것은?

> A: The machine just declined my card again.
> B: Did you try inserting instead of tapping?
> A: Yeah, I did both. Same result.
> B: Has this happened anywhere else recently?
> A: _____.
> B: Then it's probably the terminal, not your card.

① Yes, my card has been broken since last year
② No, I don't even know how a card works
③ Yes, that's why I don't use banks anymore
④ No, it worked fine at the grocery store yesterday

030 밑줄 친 부분에 들어갈 말로 가장 적절한 것은?

> The ministries of agriculture and industries have reached an agreement to _____ chicken exports to boost supply in the domestic market and help stabilize prices.

① uphold   ② purchase
③ ban   ④ endanger

028

해석 그녀는 쉬지 않고 장시간 근무한 끝에 극심한 피로를 느꼈다.

어휘 extreme 극심한 without a break 쉬지 않고 obesity 비만
vitality 활력 fatigue 피로 nutrition 영양

근거

> She experienced extreme fatigue after working long hours without a break.

정답 ③

주요 어휘 정리
fatigue 피로
= exhaustion
  tiredness
  weariness

029

> A: 기계가 또 내 카드를 거절했어.
> B: 카드를 갖다 대는 대신에 꽂아봤어?
> A: 응, 둘 다 해봤어. 결과는 똑같았어.
> B: 최근에 다른 데서도 이런 일이 있었어?
> A: 아니, 어제 식료품점에서는 잘 됐어.
> B: 그렇다면 카드가 아니라 단말기 문제일거야.

① 응, 내 카드는 작년부터 고장 났어
② 아니, 나는 카드가 어떻게 작동하는지도 몰라
③ 응, 그래서 나는 더 이상 은행을 안 써

어휘 decline 거절하다 insert 꽂다 recently 최근에
terminal 단말기

정답 ④

030

해석 농림부와 산업부는 국내시장에서의 공급을 늘리고 가격을 안정시키는 것을 돕기 위해 닭의 수출을 금지하는 합의에 도달했다.

어휘 ministry (정부의) 부 agreement 합의 boost 늘리다
domestic 국내의 stabilize 안정시키다 uphold 지지하다
purchase 구입하다 ban 금지하다 endanger 위태롭게 하다

근거

> The ministries of agriculture and industries have reached an agreement to ban chicken exports to boost supply in the domestic market and help stabilize prices.

정답 ③

주요 어휘 정리

uphold 지지하다
= support
  espouse
  buttress

ban 금지하다
= prohibit
  exclude
  forbid
  restrain
  inhibit
  proscribe
  block
  bar

031 밑줄 친 부분에 들어갈 말로 가장 적절한 것은?

> The engineer is trying to find the _____ design for the new engine because it must provide maximum efficiency with minimum cost.

① dangerous ② flexible
③ optimal   ④ ordinary

032 밑줄 친 부분에 들어갈 말로 가장 적절한 것은?

> He always dreams _____ dreams such as becoming a Superman, a Spiderman or other comic heroes.

① reasonable ② objective
③ outrageous ④ intelligent

033 밑줄 친 부분에 들어갈 말로 가장 적절한 것은?

Michael Kim
Hi, I'm messaging about the apartment for rent on Oak Street.
10:42

 Sunrise Realty
Sure! Would you be interested in coming to see it?
10:43

Michael Kim
Yes, I'd love to check it out.
10:44

 Sunrise Realty
Are you available today around 5 p.m.?
10:45

Michael Kim
That works for me. I'll be there at 5.
10:46

 Sunrise Realty
Great. Do you know how to get here?
10:47

Michael Kim
.
10:48

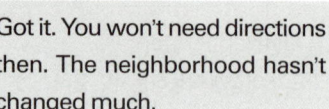 **Sunrise Realty**
Got it. You won't need directions then. The neighborhood hasn't changed much.
10:50

① No, I'm not too familiar with that area
② Yeah, I used to live nearby actually
③ Hmm, I don't have GPS in my car
④ Well, I've never been around there before

031

[해석] 기술자는 새로운 엔진에 대한 최적의 디자인을 찾으려 노력하는 데 이것은 최소의 비용으로 최고의 효율을 제공해야만 하기 때문이다.

[어휘] engineer 기술자 maximum 최고의 efficiency 효율
minimum 최소의 cost 비용 dangerous 위험한
flexible 유연한 optimal 최적의 ordinary 일반적인

[근거]
> The engineer is trying to find the optimal design for the new engine because it must provide maximum efficiency with minimum cost.

[정답] ③

주요 어휘 정리

flexible 유연한
= adaptable
  adjustable
  elastic
  resilient

optimal 최적의
= best
  ideal
  most suitable
  perfect

032

[해석] 그는 항상 슈퍼맨, 스파이더맨, 또는 다른 만화 영웅이 되는 것과 같은 터무니없는 꿈을 꾼다.

[어휘] comic 만화의 reasonable 합리적인 objective 객관적인
outrageous 터무니없는 intelligent 똑똑한

[근거]
> He always dreams outrageous dreams such as becoming a Superman, a Spiderman or other comic heroes.

[정답] ③

주요 어휘 정리

reasonable 합리적인
= rational
  sensible

outrageous 터무니없는
= ridiculous
  absurd
  nonsensical
  preposterous

033

 Michael Kim
안녕하세요, Oak Street에 있는 아파트 임대와 관련해서 연락드렸어요.
10:42

 Sunrise 부동산 중개회사
네! 아파트 보러 오실 의향 있으세요?
10:43

 Michael Kim
네, 한 번 보고 싶어요.
10:44

 Sunrise 부동산 중개회사
오늘 오후 5시쯤 괜찮으세요?
10:45

 Michael Kim
좋아요. 그때 갈게요.
10:46

 Sunrise 부동산 중개회사
좋아요. 여기 오시는 길은 아세요?
10:47

 Michael Kim
네, 사실 예전에 그 근처에 살았어요.
10:48

 Sunrise 부동산 중개회사
알겠어요. 그럼 길 안내는 필요 없겠네요. 동네는 예전이랑 많이 안 바뀌었어요.
10:50

① 아니요, 그 지역은 잘 몰라요
③ 음, 제 차에는 GPS가 없어요
④ 저기, 전 그 근처는 한 번도 가본 적 없어요

[어휘] rent 임대 realty 부동산 중개회사
be interested in ~에 관심이 있다 directions (*pl.*) 길 안내

[정답] ②

034 밑줄 친 부분에 들어갈 말로 가장 적절한 것은?

> A: Have you been following the news lately?
> B: Yeah, it's been pretty hectic. There is so much happening in the world.
> A: I know, it's hard to keep up sometimes. _____?
> B: The new environmental policies seem promising. It's about time we took action.
> A: Absolutely. I hope they make a real difference.

① Have you seen the news on polar bears
② Have you participated in ecology campaigns
③ What are your thoughts on corporal punishment
④ Any headlines that caught your attention

035 밑줄 친 부분에 들어갈 말로 가장 적절한 것은?

 Amie Lewis
Did you get the package I sent?
10:42

 Brian Murphy
No, it never arrived.
10:43

 Amie Lewis
That's strange. I sent it two days ago with express delivery.
10:44

 Brian Murphy
What address did you use?
10:45

 Amie Lewis
14-2, Saginaw Street, NC.
10:46

 Brian Murphy
Wait, I just checked the shipping confirmation email. It says NO, not NC.
10:47

 Amie Lewis
In that case, _____.
10:49

 Brian Murphy
Or maybe you just spelled it wrong.
10:50

① the abbreviation for North Carolina is NO
② the ink must have smudged during printing
③ I always make sure I spell words correctly
④ I meant NO as in "Not Ordered"

034

A: 최근에 뉴스는 계속 보고 있어?
B: 응, 다소 정신이 없어. 세상에는 너무 많은 일이 일어나고 있어.
A: 나도 알아. 때때로 따라가기 어렵지. 관심이 가는 뉴스 제목은 뭐가 있어?
B: 새로운 환경 정책들이 가능성이 높은 것 같아. 우리가 행동을 취할 때야.
A: 물론이지. 그것들이 변화를 가져오길 바라.

① 북극곰에 관한 그 뉴스 봤어
② 환경 운동에 참여한 적 있어
③ 체벌에 대한 네 생각은 뭐야

어휘 hectic 정신없는 keep up 따라가다 promising 가능성이 높은
It's about time ~할 때이다 take action 행동을 취하다
make a difference 변화를 가져오다 participate 참여하다
corporal punishment 체벌 attention 관심

정답 ④

035

Amie Lewis 10:42
내가 보낸 소포 받았어?

Brian Murphy 10:43
아니, 도착하지 않았어.

Amie Lewis 10:44
이상하네. 이틀 전에 특급 배송으로 보냈는데.

Brian Murphy 10:45
어떤 주소를 썼어?

Amie Lewis 10:46
NC, Saginaw가 14-2번지.

Brian Murphy 10:47
잠깐만, 방금 배송 확인 이메일을 확인했어. 거기엔 NC가 아니라 NO라고 적혀 있어.

Amie Lewis 10:49
그렇다면, 프린트할 때 잉크가 번졌나 봐.

Brian Murphy 10:50
아니면 네가 철자를 잘못 썼을지도 모르지.

① 노스캐롤라이나의 약자가 NO야
③ 나는 항상 단어의 철자를 정확하게 쓰려고 해
④ 나는 NO를 '주문되지 않음'이라는 의미로 썼어

어휘 express delivery 특급 배송 confirmation 확인
smudge 번지다 abbreviation 약자

정답 ②

036 밑줄 친 부분에 들어갈 말로 가장 적절한 것은?

> To reduce the possibility of infection, the doctor advised the patient to follow strict _____ after surgery.

① discipline ② hygiene
③ balance   ④ routine

037 밑줄 친 부분에 들어갈 말로 가장 적절한 것은?

Diana Barry
Hey, did you catch that new movie everyone's talking about?
10:42

Josie Pye
Yeah, I saw it last weekend. It was pretty good, actually.
10:43

Diana Barry
Nice! What did you think of the ending?
10:44

Josie Pye
I liked how they tied everything together, and I didn't expect that twist.
10:45

Diana Barry
Right? _____.
10:46

Josie Pye
Definitely. The twist was so good. We should go watch another movie together soon.
10:47

Diana Barry
Sounds like a plan.
10:49

① That's why action-comedies are popular
② The ending had too many action scenes
③ But I'm not sure the twist is necessary
④ It kept me guessing until the last scene

036

[해석] 감염의 가능성을 낮추기 위해, 의사는 환자에게 수술 후에 엄격한 위생을 지킬 것을 조언했다.

[어휘] infection 감염   strict 엄격한   surgery 수술   discipline 훈련
hygiene 위생   balance 균형   routine 일과

[근거]
> To reduce the possibility of infection, the doctor advised the patient to follow strict hygiene after surgery.

[정답] ②

[주요 어휘 정리]
hygiene 위생
= cleanliness
  sanitation

037

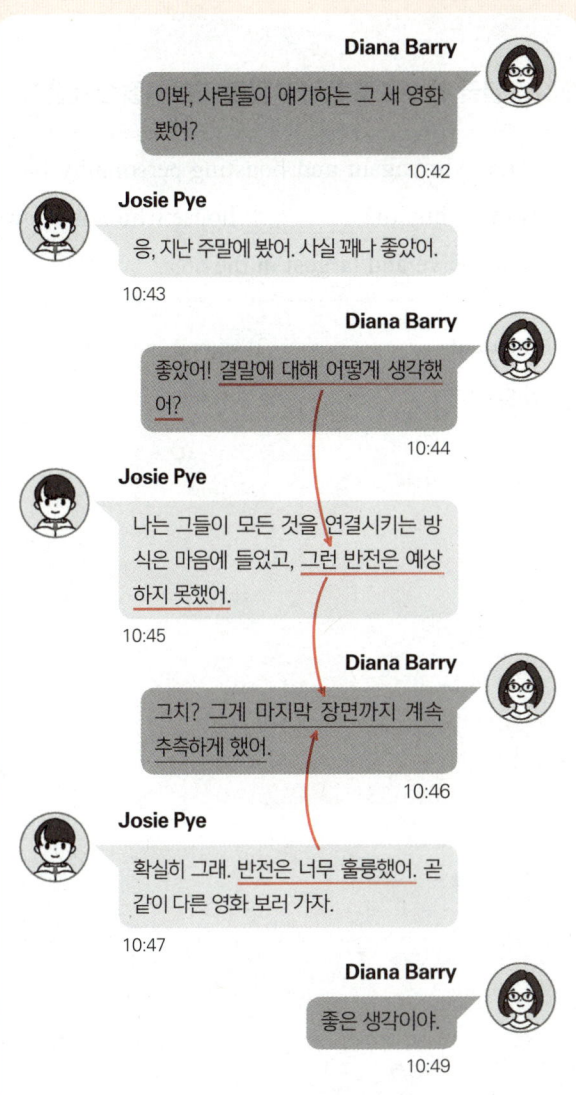

① 그게 액션 코미디가 인기 있는 이유야
② 마지막 장면은 액션 장면이 너무 많았어
③ 그런데 반전이 필요한지 확실하지 않아

[어휘] catch 보다   twist 반전   Sounds like a plan. 좋은 생각이야.
be packed with ~으로 꽉 차다   guess 추측하다

[정답] ④

DAY 04 39

038 밑줄 친 부분에 들어갈 말로 가장 적절한 것은?

> His extravagant and boasting personality has led him to buy the _____ house which is the most expensive and largest in the area.

① frugal ② sparse
③ greedy ④ lavish

039 밑줄 친 부분에 들어갈 말로 가장 적절한 것은?

> We need to learn how to repair and _____ the Earth's ozone layer so that it is no longer destroyed by human activity.

① exhaust ② replenish
③ empty ④ harness

040 밑줄 친 부분에 들어갈 말로 가장 적절한 것은?

> A: Have you been to the new fitness center downtown?
> B: Not yet. Why? Have you tried it?
> A: Yes, I signed up last month. The equipment is really modern, and they have various classes.
> B: Oh, that sounds nice. Do they offer yoga classes too?
> A: Yes, they have yoga, pilates, and even dance programs.
> B: That's awesome. I've been looking for a place like that.
> A: By the way, _____.
> B: Really? That's great. It's hard to make time on weekdays.

① the gym is open 24 hours on weekends
② the gym requires a registration fee for all classes
③ the gym has strict rules about outdoor shoes
④ the gym offers services only on weekdays

038

해석 그의 사치스럽고 자랑하는 성격은 그가 그 지역에서 가장 비싸고 큰 호화로운 집을 사도록 했다.

어휘 extravagant 사치스러운   boasting 자랑하는   personality 성격
frugal 검소한   sparse 부족한   greedy 탐욕스러운
lavish 호화로운

근거

His extravagant and boasting personality has led him to buy the lavish house which is the most expensive and largest in the area.

정답 ④

주요 어휘 정리

frugal 검소한   ↔   lavish 호화로운
= thrifty   = wasteful
  economical   prodigal
                    extravagant
                    luxurious

sparse 부족한
= scarce
  insufficient
  meager
  deficient
  lacking

039

해석 우리는 오존층이 인간 활동에 의해 더 이상 파괴되지 않도록 지구의 오존층을 복구하고 보충하는 방법을 배울 필요가 있다.

어휘 repair 복구하다   ozone layer 오존층   destroy 파괴하다
exhaust 기진맥진하게 만들다   replenish 보충하다
empty 비우다   harness 이용하다

근거

We need to learn how to repair and replenish the Earth's ozone layer so that it is no longer destroyed by human.

정답 ②

주요 어휘 정리

replenish 보충하다
= refill
  supplement
  make up for

040

A: 시내에 새로 생긴 피트니스 센터에 가 봤어?
B: 아직 안 가봤어. 왜? 넌 가 봤어?
A: 응, 난 지난달에 등록했어. 장비가 정말 최신이고 다양한 수업이 있어.
B: 좋게 들리네. 요가 수업도 제공해?
A: 응, 요가, 필라테스 심지어 댄스 프로그램이 있어.
B: 멋진데. 나도 그런 곳을 찾고 있었거든.
A: 그런데, 그 체육관은 주말에 24시간 운영해.
B: 정말? 그거 좋네. 주중에는 시간 내기가 어렵잖아.

② 그 체육관은 모든 수업에 등록금을 요구해
③ 그 체육관은 실외화에 엄격한 규정이 있어
④ 그 체육관은 오직 주중에만 서비스를 제공해

어휘 downtown 시내에   sign up 등록하다   equipment 장비
various 다양한   offer 제공하다   awesome 멋진
require 요구하다   registration fee 등록금   strict 엄격한

정답 ①

041 밑줄 친 부분에 들어갈 말로 가장 적절한 것은?

To be a good journalist, one must practice _____ such as checking facts, listening to different perspectives, and avoiding personal bias.

① honesty   ② objectivity
③ agreement   ④ emotion

042 밑줄 친 부분에 들어갈 말로 가장 적절한 것은?

Acute illnesses are usually quick and treatable, but _____ illnesses are long-term and usually require treatment for the rest of your life.

① chronic   ② adverse
③ recessive   ④ nocturnal

043 밑줄 친 부분에 들어갈 말로 가장 적절한 것은?

Rena Bradley: Hey Mark, how's it going? 10:42

Mark Spencer: I'm thinking about new career opportunities. Feeling stuck in my current job. 10:43

Rena Bradley: I get it. Did you start looking into other jobs? 10:44

Mark Spencer: Yeah, I browsed and updated my resume, but it's overwhelming. 10:45

Rena Bradley: Change can be daunting, but it's necessary for growth. _____? 10:46

Mark Spencer: I'm looking for opportunities in project management. 10:47

Rena Bradley: Good choice. I'm sure you'll find the right fit soon. 10:48

Mark Spencer: Thanks, I will keep you posted. 10:49

① What kind of role are you interested in
② Have you applied to any companies recently
③ Are you reaching out to your contacts for help
④ Why are you considering a job change

041

해석 좋은 기자가 되기 위해서는, 사실 확인, 다양한 관점 듣기, 개인적 편견 피하기와 같은 객관성을 실천해야 한다.

어휘 journalist 기사   practice 실천하다   perspective 관점
avoid 피하다   bias 편견   honesty 정직   objectivity 객관성
agreement 동의   emotion 감정

근거

> To be a good journalist, one must practice objectivity such as checking facts, listening to different perspectives, and avoiding personal bias.

정답 ②

주요 어휘 정리

honesty 정직   objectivity 객관성
= truthfulness   = impartiality
  integrity   neutrality
  sincerity   fairness

042

해석 급성 질환은 보통 순식간이고 치료할 수 있지만, 만성 질환은 장기적이고 보통 남은 평생 동안 치료를 필요로 한다.

어휘 acute 급성의   treatable 치료할 수 있는   treatment 치료
chronic 만성의   adverse 불리한   recessive 열성의
nocturnal 야행성의

근거

> Acute illnesses are usually quick and treatable, but chronic illnesses are long-term and usually require treatment for the rest of your life.

정답 ①

주요 어휘 정리

chronic 만성적인	↔	acute 급성의
adverse 불리한	↔	beneficial 유리한
recessive 열성의	↔	dominant 우성의
nocturnal 야행성의	↔	diurnal 주행성의

043

② 최근에 회사에 지원해 본 적 있니
③ 도움을 요청하기 위해 인맥들에게 연락하고 있니
④ 이직을 고려하는 이유는 무엇이니

어휘 stuck 갇힌   I get it. 알 거 같아.   look into ~을 알아보다
browse 훑어보다   resume 이력서
overwhelming 엄두가 안 나는   daunting 힘든
necessary 필요한   right fit 딱 어울리는 것
keep someone posted (최신 진행 상황을) 계속 알리다
apply 지원하다   reach out 연락하다   contact 인맥
job change 이직

정답 ①

044 밑줄 친 부분에 들어갈 말로 가장 적절한 것은?

> A: Do I need to bring anything to the party?
> B: No, you need a good mood and a smile. We've got everything covered. It's going to be a casual get-together with drinks and snacks.
> A: That sounds easy enough. When does the party start?
> B: At 7 PM. _____
> A: Got it, I'll be there around 7:30, then.
> B: Perfect! Looking forward to catching up with you.

① We're keeping it relaxed, so no rush.
② You can show up on time, right?
③ We will save a spot for you.
④ Don't be tardy for the party as usual.

045 밑줄 친 부분에 들어갈 말로 가장 적절한 것은?

Jiwon Kim
Hey, how's work going these days?
10:42

 Minho Lee
It's been kind of rough lately. Actually, I applied for a new job and had an interview yesterday.
10:43

Jiwon Kim
Really? How did that go?
10:44

 Minho Lee
The panel kept asking follow-up questions.
10:45

Jiwon Kim
That doesn't sound easy. Did you get any positive signs from them though?
10:46

 Minho Lee
Well, _____.
10:47

Jiwon Kim
That's normal after interviews. I bet you did better than you think.
10:48

① I sent them some positive signals
② I was ready for their follow-up questions
③ I walked out feeling pretty unsure
④ I got better results without putting in the work

044

> A: 파티에 뭔가를 가져가야 하나요?
> B: 아니오, 좋은 기분과 미소만 있으면 돼요. 저희가 모든 걸 책임지니까요. 술과 간식이 있는 가벼운 모임이 될 거예요.
> A: 그거 아주 괜찮네요. 파티가 언제 시작하나요?
> B: 오후 7시요. 편하게 하려고 하니까, 서두를 건 없어요.
> A: 알겠어요. 그러면, 7시 반쯤에 갈게요.
> B: 완벽하네요! 밀린 이야기를 나누길 기대할게요.

② 정시에 나타날 수 있죠, 그렇죠?
③ 당신 자리를 맡아둘게요.
④ 평소처럼 파티에 늦지 마세요.

어휘 cover 책임지다 casual 가벼운 get-together 모임
look forward to ~을 기대하다
catch up with ~와 밀린 이야기를 하다 rush 서두름
show up 나타나다 on time 정시에 tardy 늦은
as usual 평소처럼

정답 ①

045

① 그들에게 긍정적인 신호를 보냈어
② 그들의 후속 질문에 대비돼 있었어
④ 노력하지 않고 더 좋은 결과를 얻었어

어휘 rough 힘든 lately 최근에 actually 사실은
apply for ~에 지원하다 panel 면접관 follow-up 후속의
unsure 불확실한 put in the work 노력하다

정답 ③

046 밑줄 친 부분에 들어갈 말로 가장 적절한 것은?

Rachel Lynde: How's your new job going? 10:42

Ruby Gillis: It's been really interesting! I love learning new things every day. 10:43

Rachel Lynde: That's awesome. What's been the most exciting part so far? 10:44

Ruby Gillis: Definitely getting to work on new projects. 10:45

Rachel Lynde: Sounds like you're really enjoying it. 10:46

Ruby Gillis: Yeah, but _____. 10:48

Rachel Lynde: So what does he do to you? 10:49

Ruby Gillis: Well, he keeps changing priorities without notice, and it's really stressful. 10:50

① my boss has streamlined the workflow well
② my boss manages priorities effectively
③ my boss isn't as easy to work with
④ it's hard to stay focused in such a busy office

047 밑줄 친 부분에 들어갈 말로 가장 적절한 것은?

Journalism is a notoriously _____ profession. Downsizing and layoffs are almost routine, and many journalists find themselves bouncing between news organizations and periods of freelance work during their careers.

① pecuniary
② conventional
③ prolonged
④ precarious

046

① 내 상사는 업무 흐름을 잘 정리했어
② 내 상사는 우선순위를 효과적으로 정해
④ 이렇게 바쁜 사무실에서는 집중하기가 어려워

어휘 awesome 멋진   priority 우선순위   notice 공지
streamline (능률적으로) 정리하다   workflow 업무 흐름
effectively 효과적으로

정답 ③

047

해석 언론계는 악명 높게 불안정한 직업이다. 인원 감축과 정리 해고는 거의 일상적이고, 많은 기자들은 자신의 경력 동안에 언론사와 프리랜서 일을 옮겨 다니는 자신을 발견한다.

어휘 journalism 언론계   notoriously 악명 높게
profession 직업   downsizing 인원 감축   layoff 정리 해고
routine 일상적인   bounce 옮겨 다니다   pecuniary 금전상의
conventional 관습적인   prolonged 오래 계속되는
precarious 불안정한

근거

> Journalism is a notoriously precarious profession. Downsizing and layoffs are almost routine, and many journalists find themselves bouncing between news organizations and periods of freelance work during their careers.

정답 ④

주요 어휘 정리

pecuniary 금전상의   precarious 불안정한
= monetary   = insecure
  financial   unstable

048 밑줄 친 부분에 들어갈 말로 가장 적절한 것은?

> A: Hey Jack. You look tired. What's going on?
> B: It's finals week and I have been up all night studying.
> A: How many exams do you have left?
> B: Three more to go.
> A: Haven't you been keeping up your studies?
> B: _____
> A: Looks like you'll be in for a tough week.

① You are the last person to study hard.
② If you were me, would you keep up?
③ Staying up late is bad for your health.
④ If I have, wouldn't I need to stay up?

049 밑줄 친 부분에 들어갈 말로 가장 적절한 것은?

> The team initially rejected the engineer's idea because it seemed _____, but they later realized that the older method worked better than the new ones.

① resilient   ② durable
③ outdated   ④ complete

050 밑줄 친 부분에 들어갈 말로 가장 적절한 것은?

> The report highlights the _____ influence of social media on teenagers. Its effects can be seen in their language, behavior, fashion, and even sleep patterns.

① limited   ② temporary
③ harmless   ④ pervasive

048

A: 이 봐 Jack. 피곤해 보이네. 무슨 일이야?
B: 이번 주가 기말고사 주간이라 공부하느라 밤을 새우고 있어.
A: 시험이 몇 개나 남았는데?
B: 앞으로 세 개 더.
A: 공부를 꾸준히 해오지 않았어?
B: 내가 그랬으면, 밤을 새울 필요가 없지 않겠어?
A: 힘든 한 주를 보내겠구나.

① 넌 절대 열심히 공부할 사람이 아니야
② 네가 나라면, 꾸준히 하겠어?
③ 늦게까지 깨어있는 건 건강에 좋지 않아.

[어휘] keep up ~을 꾸준히 하다   tough 힘든
the last person to 절대 ~을 안 할 사람

[정답] ④

049

[해석] 그 팀은 처음에 그 엔지니어의 아이디어가 구식으로 보였기 때문에 거절했지만, 나중에는 그 오래된 방식이 새로운 방식보다 더 잘 작동한다는 것을 깨달았다.

[어휘] initially 처음에는   reject 거절하다   realize 깨닫다
resilient 회복력 있는   durable 내구성이 있는   outdated 구식의
complete 완전한

[근거]

The team initially rejected the engineer's idea because it seemed outdated, but they later realized that the older method worked better than the new ones.

[정답] ③

[주요 어휘 정리]
durable 내구성이 있는   outdated 구식의, 시대에 뒤떨어진
= lasting   = old-fashioned
  sturdy   obsolete
  strong   antiquated

050

[해석] 보고서는 소셜 미디어의 청소년에 미치는 만연한 영향을 강조한다. 소셜 미디어의 영향은 그들의 언어, 행동, 패션, 심지어 수면 형태에서 보여질 수 있다.

[어휘] highlight 강조하다   influence 영향   effect 영향
limited 제한된   temporary 임시의   harmless 무해한
pervasive 만연한

[근거]

The report highlights the pervasive influence of social media on teenagers. Its effects can be seen in their language, behavior, fashion, and even sleep patterns.

[정답] ④

[주요 어휘 정리]
temporary 일시적인   pervasive 만연한
= momentary   = widespread
  short-term   prevalent
  brief   omnipresent
  tentative   ubiquitous
  provisional

DAY 05

051 밑줄 친 부분에 들어갈 말로 가장 적절한 것은?

> The final proposal to meet the original objection to radical changes claims that alterations will be made through a _____ process, not all at once.

① extensive ② limited
③ rapid   ④ gradual

052 밑줄 친 부분에 들어갈 말로 가장 적절한 것은?

> Plants absorb essential _____ from the soil to maintain healthy growth, much like animals rely on a balanced diet for nourishment.

① symptoms   ② contaminants
③ pesticides ④ nutrients

053 밑줄 친 부분에 들어갈 말로 가장 적절한 것은?

Jamie Belle
I want to go on an international trip for the next vacation. Do you have any suggestions?
10:42

Brian Adams
How about Europe? Paris or Rome would be amazing.
10:43

Jamie Belle
That's a great idea! I'd love to see the Eiffel Tower in Paris.
10:44

Brian Adams
Exactly, and in Rome, you should definitely visit the Colosseum.
10:45

Jamie Belle
_____. My summer vacation is only one week long.
10:46

Brian Adams
In that case, how about Japan or Taiwan? They're closer and still offer wonderful travel experiences.
10:47

Jamie Belle
Sounds good! Tokyo in Japan or Taipei in Taiwan both seem exciting!
10:48

① But I'm so into Western culture
② Besides, I'm accompanied by my mother
③ But Europe is too far to travel
④ On top of that, I like adventures

051

해석 급진적인 변화에 대한 최초의 반대를 충족하는 최종 계획은 변경이 한꺼번에 아니라 점진적인 과정을 통해 이루어질 것이라고 주장한다.

어휘 proposal 계획　objection 반대　radical 급진적인
claim 주장하다　alteration 변화　process 과정
all at once 한꺼번에　extensive 광범위한　limited 제한적인
rapid 빠른　gradual 점진적인

근거
> The final proposal to meet the original objection to radical changes claims that alterations will be made through a gradual process, not all at once.

정답 ④

주요 어휘 정리
gradual 점진적인, 서서히 하는
= moderate
　unhurried
　progressive
　steady

052

해석 동물이 영양을 위해 균형 잡힌 식단에 의존하는 것과 매우 유사하게 식물은 건강한 성장을 유지하기 위해 토양으로부터 필수 영양소를 흡수한다.

어휘 absorb 흡수하다　essential 필수적인　soil 토양
maintain 유지하다　healthy 건강한　growth 성장
balanced 균형 잡힌　diet 식단　nourishment 영양
symptom 증상　contaminant 오염 물질　pesticide 살충제
nutrient 영양소

근거
> Plants absorb essential nutrients from the soil to maintain healthy growth, much like animals rely on a balanced diet for nourishment.

정답 ④

주요 어휘 정리
nutrient 영양
= nourishment
　nutrition

053

① 하지만 저는 서구 문화에 푹 빠져 있어요
② 게다가, 저는 어머니와 동행해요
④ 그뿐 아니라, 저는 모험을 좋아해요

어휘 international trip 해외여행　suggestion 제안
be into ~에 빠지다　accompany 동행하다　on top of ~뿐 아니라
adventure 모험

정답 ③

054 밑줄 친 부분에 들어갈 말로 가장 적절한 것은?

> He was greeted with the warm and _____ welcome when his name was read out.

① passive   ② hospitable
③ hostile   ④ confidential

055 밑줄 친 부분에 들어갈 말로 가장 적절한 것은?

> At one point, she experienced a serious injury that could have _____ her career.

① enhanced   ② jeopardized
③ maintained ④ endorsed

056 밑줄 친 부분에 들어갈 말로 가장 적절한 것은?

> A: I'm really worried about this project. Nothing is going as planned.
> B: Don't stress too much. I'm sure we can sort it out.
> A: By the way, I can't make it at 11 PM for our meeting. Can we reschedule?
> B: No problem! When would be better for you?
> A: Sometime tomorrow morning? But above all, _____.
> B: Yeah, let's talk it through later. I'm confident we can reach an agreement.

① honestly, I haven't really looked into the project yet
② I don't think it's a good idea to put off this conversation
③ the issue is that we disagree with each other
④ I'm not sure if I'm the right person for this

054

해석 그의 이름이 불렸을 때 그는 따뜻하고 친절한 환영을 받았다.

어휘 greet 환영하다 read out 부르다 passive 수동적인
hospitable 친절한 hostile 호전적인 confidential 비밀의

근거

> He was greeted with the warm and hospitable welcome when his name was read out.

정답 ②

주요 어휘 정리

hospitable 친절한, 환대하는		hostile 호전적인, 적대적인	
= welcoming	friendly	= warlike	belligerent
agreeable	congenial	antagonistic	bellicose
affable	genial	aggressive	inimical
amiable	cordial		
amicable			

055

해석 한때 그녀는 자기 경력을 위태롭게 할 수도 있었던 심각한 부상을 경험했다.

어휘 serious 심각한 injury 부상 career 경력 enhance 향상시키다
jeopardize 위태롭게 하다 maintain 유지하다
endorse 지지하다

근거

> At one point, she experienced a serious injury that could have jeopardized her career.

정답 ②

주요 어휘 정리

jeopardize 위태롭게 하다	endorse 지지하다
= threaten	= support
endanger	advocate
imperil	uphold
risk	champion

056

> A: 이 프로젝트 정말 걱정돼. 아무것도 계획대로 안 되고 있어.
> B: 너무 스트레스받지 마. 분명 해결할 수 있을 거야.
> A: 그런데 말이야, 우리 11시에 있는 회의엔 못 갈 것 같아. 다시 일정 잡을 수 있을까?
> B: 문제없어! 언제가 더 괜찮아?
> A: 내일 아침쯤? 하지만 무엇보다, 문제는 우리 둘의 의견이 다르다는 거야.
> B: 응, 나중에 충분히 얘기해보자. 합의에 도달할 수 있을 거라고 자신해.

① 솔직히 아직 그 프로젝트에 대해 제대로 살펴보지 않았어
② 이 대화를 미루는 건 좋지 않은 것 같아
④ 제가 이 일에 적합한 사람인지 잘 모르겠어

어휘 stress 스트레스 받다 sort out ~을 해결하다
make it (모임에) 가다 reschedule 일정을 다시 잡다
talk it through (문제나 상황에 대해) 충분히 이야기하다
confident 자신하는 agreement 합의 honestly 솔직히
look into ~을 살펴보다

정답 ③

057 밑줄 친 부분에 들어갈 말로 가장 적절한 것은?

A: Are we still planning to launch the beta version next Friday?
B: That was the plan, but we hit a few bugs during testing.
A: Is it serious enough to delay the release?
B: _____.
A: Then we should let the marketing team know today.
B: Agreed. No point in promoting a product that won't be ready.

① It's mostly minor, so I think we can go ahead
② We actually resolved all of them last night
③ Possibly. We haven't figured out the root cause yet
④ We already posted the release announcement

058 밑줄 친 부분에 들어갈 말로 가장 적절한 것은?

Peter Singer
Mr. Stevens' flight is coming in 30 minutes early this afternoon. I'm heading to pick him up.
10:42

 Amy Jones
Our team is thrilled he's finally joining us. Is everything set for his welcome meeting?
10:43

Peter Singer
Yes, we've booked the conference room and prepared the agenda.
10:44

 Amy Jones
Perfect. I'll ensure the welcome packet and his office are ready. Anything else?
10:45

Peter Singer
_____?
10:46

 Amy Jones
Sure, I'll confirm with the IT team right away.
10:47

Peter Singer
Please write down his ID and temporary password.
10:49

① Is his office still under renovations
② Do you have any requests for his office setup
③ Are you aware of his employment conditions
④ Could you check his email has been set up

057

> A: 우리 여전히 다음 주 금요일에 베타 버전 출시하는 거지?
> B: 원래 그랬는데 테스트 중에 버그가 좀 나왔어.
> A: 출시를 미룰 정도로 심각한 건가?
> B: 그럴 수도 있어. 근본 원인을 아직 파악 못 했어.
> A: 그럼 마케팅팀한테 오늘 안으로 알려야겠네.
> B: 동의해. 준비가 안 된 걸 홍보해 봐야 소용없지.

① 대부분 사소해서, 그냥 진행해도 될 것 같아
② 사실 어젯밤에 전부 해결했어
④ 우리 이미 출시 공지를 게시했어

어휘 launch 출시하다 delay 미루다 release 출시
promote 홍보하다 mostly 대부분 minor 사소한
go ahead 진행하다 resolve 해결하다 figure out 파악하다
root cause 근본 원인 post 게시하다 announcement 공지

정답 ③

058

① 그의 사무실이 아직도 수리 중인가요
② 그의 사무실 설정에 대해 요청할 게 있나요
③ 그의 고용 조건을 알고 계시나요

어휘 head 가다 pick up (자동차로) 마중을 나가다 thrilled 신이 난
conference room 회의실 agenda 안건 ensure 확실하게 하다
packet (선물) 꾸러미 confirm 확인하다 renovation 수리
be aware of ~을 알다 employment 고용 condition 조건

정답 ④

059 밑줄 친 부분에 들어갈 말로 가장 적절한 것은?

Olivia Morgan
Hi, I'm having trouble logging into my account.
10:42

Support Agent
I'm sorry to hear that. Could you please tell me what seems to be the issue?
10:43

Olivia Morgan
It keeps saying my password is incorrect, but I'm sure it's right.
10:44

Support Agent
I see. Let me check your account details.
10:45

Olivia Morgan
Sure, I appreciate your help.
10:46

Support Agent
Alright, _____.
10:47

Olivia Morgan
Oh, okay. What should I do next?
10:48

Support Agent
You should've received a reset email just now. Please follow the link to set a new password.
10:49

① I've reset your password
② I've canceled your subscription
③ your delivery will arrive tomorrow
④ but there's nothing else we can do right now

060 밑줄 친 부분에 들어갈 말로 가장 적절한 것은?

> The volcano had been _____ for centuries, but suddenly showed signs of activity with small tremors and minor eruptions.

① distant
② nocturnal
③ active
④ dormant

059

② 제가 구독을 취소해드렸습니다
③ 택배는 내일 도착할 것입니다
④ 하지만 지금 당장 저희가 할 수 있는 다른 것이 없습니다

[어휘] **have trouble -ing** ~하는 데 문제가 있다　**keep -ing** 계속 ~하다
account details 계정 정보　**appreciate** 감사하다
reset 재설정; 재설정하다　**just now** 방금　**cancel** 취소하다
subscription 구독　**delivery** 택배

[정답] ①

060

[해석] 그 화산은 수 세기 동안 휴면 상태였으나 갑자기 작은 진동과 작은 분출로 활동 징후를 보였다.

[어휘] **volcano** 화산　**century** 세기　**sign** 징후　**tremor** 진동
minor 작은　**eruption** 분출　**distant** 먼　**nocturnal** 야행성의
active 활동적인　**dormant** 휴면의

[근거]

> The volcano had been dormant for centuries, but suddenly showed signs of activity with small tremors and minor eruptions.

[정답] ④

[주요 어휘 정리]

distant 먼	dormant 휴면의
= far	= inactive
remote	inert
	static
	stagnant
	sedentary

061 밑줄 친 부분에 들어갈 말로 가장 적절한 것은?

> When a company sells products to another business, it usually sends a(n) _____ to request payment and provide details of the transaction.

① souvenir ② abstract
③ license ④ invoice

062 밑줄 친 부분에 들어갈 말로 가장 적절한 것은?

> The scientist found the region to be _____ in natural resources, which could support the local economy.

① abundant ② scarce
③ insufficient ④ humid

063 밑줄 친 부분에 들어갈 말로 가장 적절한 것은?

Gilbert Blythe
How long in advance can I book a meeting room for?
10:42

Nancy Sloan
Meetings may be scheduled up to 4 weeks in advance.
10:43

Gilbert Blythe
Then, I want to schedule a meeting for September 9th.
10:44

Nancy Sloan
Let me see, oh, that day is fully booked.
10:45

Gilbert Blythe
Oh, no! _____
_____
10:46

Nancy Sloan
You can sign up for alerts, and you'll get an automated message if a reservation spot opens up.
10:47

① Do you think now is as good time as any?
② I have a very tight schedule on that day.
③ Can you notify me if there is an opening?
④ I think I can reschedule it for October 9th.

061

[해석] 회사가 다른 업체에 제품을 판매할 때, 대금을 청구하고 거래 내역을 제공하기 위해 보통 송장을 보낸다.

[어휘] transaction 거래   souvenir 기념품   abstract 개요
license 면허증   invoice 송장

[근거]
When a company sells products to another business, it usually sends an invoice to request payment and provide details of the transaction.

[정답] ④

[주요 어휘 정리]
invoice 송장
= bill
  statement

062

[해석] 그 과학자는 그 지역이 천연자원이 풍부하다는 것을 발견했는데, 그것은 지역 경제를 부양할 수 있었다.

[어휘] region 지역   natural resource 천연자원   support 부양하다
abundant 풍부한   scarce 부족한   insufficient 불충분한
humid 습한

[근거]
The scientist found the region to be abundant in natural resources, which could support the local economy.

[정답] ①

[주요 어휘 정리]
abundant 풍부한	insufficient 불충분한
= rich	= inadequate
plentiful	deficient
fertile	sparse
bountiful	scarce
ample	lacking
exuberant	short

063

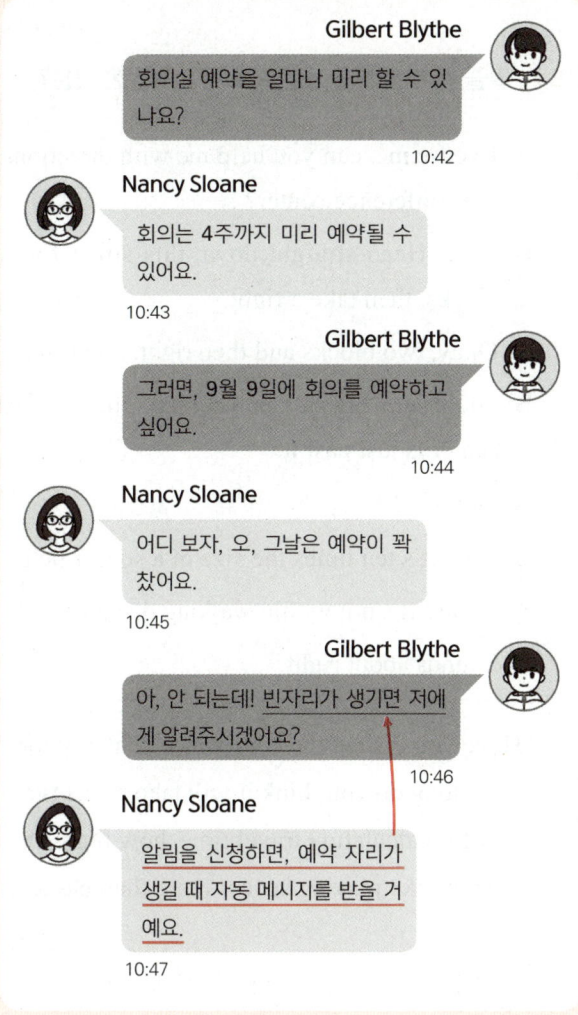

① 지금이 가장 좋은 시기라고 생각하세요?
② 저는 그날 일정이 아주 꽉 찼어요.
④ 10월 9일로 일정을 다시 잡아도 될 것 같아요.

[어휘] book 예약하다   in advance 미리   sign up for ~을 신청하다
alert 알림   reservation 예약   notify 알리다

[정답] ③

064 밑줄 친 부분에 들어갈 말로 가장 적절한 것은?

A: Excuse me, can you help me with directions to the conference center?

B: Sure! Head straight down this street for two blocks, then take a right.

A: Okay, two blocks and then right. After that?

B: You'll see a big park on your left. The conference center is just past it.

A: Got it. _____?

B: Uhh, it's ten times the size of a soccer field.

A: What? It's not within walking distance.

B: Sounds about right.

① Have you visited the conference center before
② How long do you think it will take to get there
③ Just for calculating travel time, how big is the park
④ Do you like playing soccer more than basketball

065 밑줄 친 부분에 들어갈 말로 가장 적절한 것은?

Michael Park
Hey, are you ready for the presentation?
10:42

 Sophia Lee
It's all set. I checked everything yesterday.
10:43

Michael Park
Good to hear! Then, _____?
10:44

 Sophia Lee
What? I thought it was Amber Hall.
10:45

Michael Park
It will be held in the Echo Room. The decision was made this morning.
10:46

 Sophia Lee
Phew, I would be in big trouble if you didn't mention it.
10:47

① do you know how to get to Amber Hall
② did you hear the venue has changed
③ do you need anything else besides the projector
④ will you let me know if there are any further updates

064

A: 실례합니다. 컨퍼런스 센터로 가는 길을 알려주시겠어요?
B: 물론이죠! 이 길을 따라 두 블록 정도 직진한 후 우회전하세요.
A: 좋아요, 두 블록을 지나 오른쪽으로요. 그다음은요?
B: 왼쪽에 큰 공원이 보일 거예요. 컨퍼런스 센터는 그곳을 지나면 있습니다.
A: 알겠습니다. 그저 이동 시간을 계산하려고 그러는데요, 공원이 얼마나 큰가요?
B: 어, 축구장의 열 배 크기에요.
A: 네? 걸을 수 있는 거리는 아니네요.
B: 아마 그럴 것 같네요.

① 컨퍼런스 센터를 예전에 방문한 적이 있나요
② 그곳에 도착하기까지 시간이 얼마나 걸릴까요
④ 농구보다 축구 하는 것을 더 좋아하시나요

어휘 directions (pl.) 길 head 가다
within walking distance 걸을 수 있는 거리에
calculate 계산하다 travel time 이동 시간

정답 ③

065

① Amber Hall에 어떻게 가는지 알아
③ 프로젝터 말고 또 필요한 거 있어
④ 추가 업데이트가 있으면 알려줄래

어휘 all set 다 준비된 mention 말하다 venue 장소

정답 ②

066 밑줄 친 부분에 들어갈 말로 가장 적절한 것은?

Anna Taylor
Hey, Tim, I just got word that the project deadline has been moved up to Friday.
10:42

 Tim Evans
Oh wow, that's sooner than expected.
10:43

Anna Taylor
Right, we didn't see that coming.
10:44

 Tim Evans
Do we need to adjust our schedule?
10:45

Anna Taylor
Yes, let's reschedule the team meeting to tomorrow morning to discuss it.
10:46

 Tim Evans
Got it.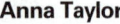
Anything else?
10:47

Anna Taylor
That should cover it for now. Thanks, Tim!
10:48

① What is the agenda for tomorrow's meeting?
② I'll send out the new meeting invite.
③ Where should we meet?
④ Our schedule has been delayed.

067 밑줄 친 부분에 들어갈 말로 가장 적절한 것은?

While using the tool may be _____ at first, persistent practice will help you use it to your advantage.

① convenient   ② awkward
③ comfortable ④ beneficial

068 밑줄 친 부분에 들어갈 말로 가장 적절한 것은?

After searching the entire park for hours, he realized he couldn't _____ his lost wallet and reluctantly decided to give up.

① retrieve   ② extract
③ irrigate   ④ discharge

066

① 내일 회의 안건은 무엇인가요?
③ 어디서 만날까요?
④ 저희 일정이 지연되었습니다.

[어휘] move up (일정을) 앞당기다   adjust 조정하다
cover 충분히 다루다   agenda 안건   send out 보내다
invite 초대장   delay 연기하다

[정답] ②

067

[해석] 처음에는 그 도구를 사용하는 것이 서투를 수 있지만, 지속적인 연습은 그것을 당신에게 유리하게 사용할 수 있도록 도와줄 것이다.

[어휘] tool 도구   persistent 지속적인   practice 연습
to one's advantage (~에게) 유리하게   convenient 편리한
awkward 서투른   comfortable 편안한   beneficial 유익한

[근거]
While using the tool may be awkward at first, persistent practice will help you use it to your advantage.

[정답] ②

[주요 어휘 정리]
awkward 서투른
= unskilled
  clumsy
  inept

068

[해석] 몇 시간 동안 공원 전체를 찾아본 후, 그는 잃어버린 지갑을 되찾을 수 없다는 것을 깨닫고 마지못해 포기하기로 결정했다.

[어휘] entire 전체의   realize 깨닫다   wallet 지갑
reluctantly 마지못해   give up 포기하다   retrieve 되찾다
extract 발췌하다   irrigate (땅에) 물을 대다   discharge 방출하다

[근거]
After searching the entire park for hours, he realized he couldn't retrieve his lost wallet and reluctantly decided to give up.

[정답] ①

[주요 어휘 정리]
retrieve 되찾다
= recover
  restore
  revitalize
  get back

069 밑줄 친 부분에 들어갈 말로 가장 적절한 것은?

> A: I thought you said you were going to call me last night.
> B: I did, but I got caught up with work and lost track of time.
> A: No worries, I was just wondering what happened.
> B: Actually, there was a reason for it. _____ _____.
> A: Wow, congratulations! How about we celebrate this weekend?
> B: Definitely! Let's make plans.

① I didn't think it was important to you
② I was hoping you would call me first
③ I thought it'd be fun to have it be a surprise
④ I got a promotion, which made me so busy

070 밑줄 친 부분에 들어갈 말로 가장 적절한 것은?

> The policy was intended to create a more _____ workplace, but in reality, it has only increased hostility among employees, driving them further apart.

① solitary
② competitive
③ isolated
④ harmonious

069

A: 어젯밤에 네가 나에게 전화한다고 말했던 것 같은데.
B: 그랬지, 그런데 일에 빠져서 시간 가는 줄 몰랐어.
A: 괜찮아, 단지 무슨 일 생겼는지 궁금했을 뿐이야.
B: 실은, 그럴 만한 이유가 있었어. 나 승진했어, 그래서 너무 바빴어.
A: 와우, 축하해! 이번 주말에 우리 축하하는 것이 어떨까?
B: 물론이지! 계획을 짜자.

① 그것이 너에게 중요하다고 생각하지 않았어
② 네가 나에게 먼저 전화할 거라 기대하고 있었어
③ 깜짝 놀라게 하면 재미있을 것 같았어

[어휘] get caught up with ~에 빠져 있다
lose track of time 시간 가는 줄 모르다 No worries. 괜찮아.
celebrate 축하하다 promotion 승진

[정답] ④

070

[해석] 그 정책은 더 조화로운 직장을 만들기 위해 의도되었지만, 실제로는 직원들 사이의 적대감을 키우고 그들이 더 멀어지게 할 뿐이었다.

[어휘] policy 정책 hostility 적대감 solitary 혼자의
competitive 경쟁적인 isolated 고립된 harmonious 조화로운

[근거]
The policy was intended to create a more harmonious workplace, but in reality, it has only increased hostility among employees, driving them further apart.

[정답] ④

주요 어휘 정리

solitary 혼자의	harmonious 조화로운
= lonely	= amicable
single	friendly
alone	cooperative

071 밑줄 친 부분에 들어갈 말로 가장 적절한 것은?

> A: Did you see the files I left on your desk?
> B: Yes, but some pages are missing.
> A: Really? I thought I printed everything.
> B: Well, I couldn't find the last section.
> A: Oh, _____?
> B: Not yet. I'll take a look at it.

① did you check the printer tray
② should I print them again for you
③ do you want me to look for them
④ could you have thrown them away by mistake

072 밑줄 친 부분에 들어갈 말로 가장 적절한 것은?

Kelly Parker
Willy, what are you doing?
10:42

Willy Adams
Hi, Kelly! I'm making plans to run for president of the student council.
10:43

Kelly Parker
Wow, that sounds like a lot of work.
10:44

Willy Adams
Yeah, there's so much to do. I really hope my friends help me out.
10:45

Kelly Parker
I want to help. Is there anything I can do?
10:47

Willy Adams
You got first prize in the drawing contest, didn't you?
10:48

Kelly Parker
Yeah, but how can that help you?
10:50

Willy Adams
_____.
10:51

① Let's invite other students to our club
② You can make election campaign posters for me
③ Don't worry, I'll vote against her in this election
④ Please check if she runs for student council president

071

> A: 내가 네 책상에 놔둔 파일 봤어?
> B: 응, 그런데 몇 페이지가 없어.
> A: 정말? 다 출력한 줄 알았는데.
> B: 글쎄, 마지막 부분을 못 찾았어.
> A: 오, 프린터함 확인해봤어?
> B: 아직 못했어. 거길 살펴볼게.

② 내가 다시 출력해줄까
③ 내가 찾아봐줄까
④ 네가 실수로 버렸을 수도 있을까

어휘 section 부분 take a look at ~을 살펴보다
throw away ~을 버리다   by mistake 실수로

정답 ①

072

① 다른 학생들을 우리 동아리에 초대하자
③ 걱정하지 마, 나는 이번 선거에서 그녀에게 반대하는 투표를 할 거야
④ 그녀가 학생회장 선거에 출마하는지 확인해줘

어휘 president 회장 student council 학생회 run for ~에 출마하다
invite 초대하다 election 선거 vote 투표하다
against ~에 반대하는

정답 ②

073 밑줄 친 부분에 들어갈 말로 가장 적절한 것은?

> The teacher encouraged the students to be more _____ by sharing their ideas and opinions during class discussions.

① reserved ② assertive
③ hesitant ④ passive

074 밑줄 친 부분에 들어갈 말로 가장 적절한 것은?

> Detectives _____ the suspect's movements by carefully following and recording each step using security camera footage.

① discard ② trace
③ nourish ④ miss

075 밑줄 친 부분에 들어갈 말로 가장 적절한 것은?

> A: How's your new job going so far?
> B: It's been a bit tricky.
> A: I was expecting an opposite answer. Aren't you doing the same sort of work as you did before?
> B: You're right, but _____.
> A: Well, relationship can be harder than work itself.
> B: I can't agree with you more.

① I get along well with people around me
② I think I'm confident in my role already
③ I have a problem with coworkers
④ I'm so used to the atmosphere at the company

073

해석 선생님은 학생들이 수업 토론 시간에 자신의 생각과 의견을 공유함으로써 더 적극적이도록 격려했다.

어휘 encourage 격려하다   discussion 토론   reserved 내성적인
assertive 적극적인   hesitant 주저하는   passive 수동적인

근거

> The teacher encouraged the students to be more assertive by sharing their ideas and opinions during class discussions.

정답 ②

주요 어휘 정리

reserved 내성적인, 말을 잘 하지 않는   hesitant 꺼리는, 주저하는
= reticent   = reluctant
  quiet   unwilling
  uncommunicative

passive 소극적인, 수동적인
= inactive

074

해석 형사들은 보안 카메라 화면을 이용해 각 단계를 신중하게 따라가고 기록함으로써 용의자의 움직임을 추적한다.

어휘 detective 형사   suspect 용의자   movement 움직임
security 보안   footage (특정한 사건을 담은) 화면   discard 버리다   trace 추적하다   nourish 양육하다   miss 놓치다

근거

> Detectives trace the suspect's movements by carefully following and recording each step using security camera footage.

정답 ②

주요 어휘 정리

discard 버리다   trace 추적하다
= abandon   = track
  desert   monitor
  dump   follow
  do away with
  dispose of

075

> A: 새 직장은 지금까지 어때요?
> B: 좀 까다로워요.
> A: 저는 반대의 대답을 기대하고 있었는데요. 전에 하던 것과 같은 종류의 일을 하시는 거 아니에요?
> B: 그건 그렇지만, 동료들과 문제가 있어요.
> A: 흠, 인간관계가 일 자체보다 더 어려울 수 있죠.
> B: 전적으로 동의해요.

① 저는 주변 사람들과 잘 지내요
② 저는 벌써 새 직무에 자신감이 생기는 거 같아요
④ 저는 회사 분위기에 정말 익숙해요

어휘 so far 지금까지   tricky 까다로운   opposite 반대의
relationship 인간관계
I can't agree with you more. 전적으로 동의해요.
get along with ~와 잘 지내다   confident 자신감이 있는
coworker 동료   atmosphere 분위기

정답 ③

DAY 08

076 밑줄 친 부분에 들어갈 말로 가장 적절한 것은?

Many diseases present a variety of _____, such as fever, coughing, and fatigue, making accurate diagnosis essential for effective treatment.

① remedies ② symptoms
③ outcomes ④ recoveries

077 밑줄 친 부분에 들어갈 말로 가장 적절한 것은?

The organization will launch numerous projects to _____ forests in these countries. They will be very helpful to protect the soil from being eroded by wind and rain.

① preserve ② destroy
③ prepare ④ damage

078 밑줄 친 부분에 들어갈 말로 가장 적절한 것은?

Daniel Smith
I heard that you were recently promoted to project manager. Congratulations!
10:42

Rachel Kim
Thank you very much. I am doing my best to adjust to the new role.
10:43

Daniel Smith
I truly envy you. _____.
10:44

Rachel Kim
Please do not feel discouraged. Your time will come sooner or later.
10:45

Daniel Smith
You are right. I will make a fresh start.
10:46

Rachel Kim
That is exactly the mindset you need. Let us both keep doing our best.
10:47

① I promoted one of my team members last week
② Promotions usually come with too much responsibility
③ I declined a promotion offer last month
④ I have been passed over for a promotion several times

076

해석 많은 질병은 발열, 기침, 피로와 같은 다양한 증상을 나타내기 때문에, 정확한 진단이 효과적인 치료에 필수적이다.

어휘 disease 질병 present (질병이 증상을) 나타내다
a variety of 다양한 fatigue 피로 accurate 정확한
diagnosis 진단 essential 필수적인 effective 효과적인
treatment 치료 remedy 치료약 symptom 증상
outcome 결과 recovery 회복

근거

Many diseases present a variety of symptoms, such as fever, coughing, and fatigue, making accurate diagnosis essential for effective treatment.

정답 ②

주요 어휘 정리

remedy 치료	outcome 결과, 성과
= treatment	= result
	effect
	consequence

077

해석 그 단체는 이 국가들의 숲을 보존하기 위한 수많은 프로젝트를 시작할 것이다. 그것들은 바람과 비에 침식되고 있는 토양을 보호하는 데 매우 도움이 될 것이다.

어휘 organization 단체 launch 시작하다 numerous 수많은
protect 보호하다 soil 토양 erode 침식시키다
preserve 보존하다 destroy 파괴하다 prepare 준비하다
damage 피해를 주다

근거

The organization will launch numerous projects to preserve forests in these countries. They will be very helpful to protect the soil from being eroded by wind and rain.

정답 ①

주요 어휘 정리

preserve 보존하다	destroy 파괴하다
= conserve	= demolish
maintain	ruin
protect	wreck
sustain	devastate
shield	
safeguard	

078

① 지난주에 제 팀원 중 한 명을 승진시켰어요
② 승진은 보통 너무 많은 책임이 따르더라고요
③ 지난달에 승진 제안을 거절했어요

어휘 recently 최근에 promote 승진시키다 adjust 적응하다
discouraged 낙담한 sooner or later 조만간 exactly 정확히
mindset 마음가짐 promotion 승진 responsibility 책임
decline 거절하다 pass over (승진에서) 제외시키다

정답 ④

079 밑줄 친 부분에 들어갈 말로 가장 적절한 것은?

> Instead of _____ any important data, make sure you include all relevant information when preparing the report to influence the final decision.

① covering ② grasping
③ involving ④ omitting

080 밑줄 친 부분에 들어갈 말로 가장 적절한 것은?

Diamond Sports Center
Hello, Diamond Sports Center. May I help you?
10:42

Katie Walker
Hello. I'm Katie Walker, and a member of your sports center. I want to know if I can suspend my membership.
10:43

Diamond Sports Center
Okay, you mean you can't come for a while?
10:44

Katie Walker
That's right. I broke my leg yesterday.
10:45

Diamond Sports Center
Oh, I'm sorry. You can put your membership on hold for up to 60 days.
10:46

Katie Walker
_____
The doctor said it would take me at least 3 months to get back to normal.
10:47

Diamond Sports Center
We can bend the rules for you if you submit a medical certificate.
10:48

Katie Walker
Thank you, I'll send it right away.
10:49

① When can I get a full physical examination?
② I'll be able to start again after two months.
③ Why don't you stick to the regulations?
④ I'm sorry, but I need a further suspension.

079

[해석] 최종 결정에 영향을 미치기 위해 보고서를 준비할 때 중요한 자료를 제외시키는 대신 모든 관련 정보를 반드시 포함해야 한다.

[어휘] make sure 반드시 ~하다   include 포함하다   relevant 관련된
influence 영향을 주다   cover 다루다   grasp 파악하다
involve 포함하다   omit 제외시키다

[근거]
Instead of omitting any important data, make sure you include all relevant information when preparing the report to influence the final decision.

[정답] ④

[주요 어휘 정리]
involve 포함시키다   omit 제외시키다
= contain   = leave out
  cover
  incorporate
  include

080

Diamond Sports Center
안녕하세요, Diamond 스포츠 센터입니다. 무엇을 도와드릴까요?
10:42

 Katie Walker
안녕하세요. 저는 Katie Walker 이고, 귀하의 스포츠 센터 회원입니다. 제 회원권을 일시 중지할 수 있는지 알고 싶어요.
10:43

Diamond Sports Center
네, 당분간 못 오신다는 말씀이신가요?
10:44

 Katie Walker
맞아요. 어제 다리가 부러졌거든요.
10:45

Diamond Sports Center
아, 유감이네요. 최대 60일까지 회원권을 일시 중지할 수 있어요.
10:46

 Katie Walker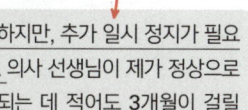
죄송하지만, 추가 일시 정지가 필요해요. 의사 선생님이 제가 정상으로 회복되는 데 적어도 3개월이 걸릴 거라고 하셨거든요.
10:47

Diamond Sports Center
진단서를 제출하시면 편의를 봐 드릴 수 있어요.
10:48

 Katie Walker
감사합니다, 당장 보낼게요.
10:49

① 제가 종합 건강 검진을 언제 받을 수 있나요?
② 두 달 뒤에 다시 시작할 수 있을 거예요.
③ 규칙을 지키는 게 어때요?

[어휘] suspend 일시 중지하다   membership 회원권
for a while 당분간   break one's leg 다리가 부러지다
put ~ on hold ~을 일시 중지하다   bend the rules 편의를 봐주다
submit 제출하다   medical certificate 진단서
full physical examination 종합 건강 검진   stick to ~을 지키다
regulations 규칙   suspension 일시 중지

[정답] ④

081 밑줄 친 부분에 들어갈 말로 가장 적절한 것은?

> The war prisoners were imprisoned in 10 _____ camps, later to be moved to permanent relocation centers.

① perpetual ② temporary
③ severe   ④ valid

082 밑줄 친 부분에 들어갈 말로 가장 적절한 것은?

> A: I think we've made good progress on the project today.
> B: Agreed, we've covered a lot of ground.
> A: _____?
> B: Not that I can think of. Everything is going right.
> A: Sounds good! Then let's finish for today.
> B: Great. See you tomorrow!

① Did we receive the shipment of office supplies
② Did we resolve all the issues related to it
③ Have you finished your performance review
④ Is there anything else we need to finalize

083 밑줄 친 부분에 들어갈 말로 가장 적절한 것은?

> The training program was designed to make employees more _____ in handling emergencies, but many still felt unprepared and unsure of what to do.

① confident ② hesitant
③ anxious   ④ reluctant

081

해석 전쟁 포로들은 10개의 임시 수용소에 수감되었고, 이후 영구적인 강제 수용소로 옮겨졌다.

어휘 prisoner 포로   imprison 수감하다
relocation camp 강제 수용소   permanent 영구적인
perpetual 끊임없이 계속되는   temporary 임시의   severe 엄격한
valid 유효한

근거

> The war prisoners were imprisoned in 10 temporary camps, later to be moved to permanent relocation centers.

정답 ②

주요 어휘 정리

perpetual 영원한 ↔ temporary 임시의
= permanent   = provisional
  perennial   momentary
  persistent   transient
  eternal   transitory
  everlasting   tentative
  incessant   evanescent
  ceaseless   ephemeral
  unceasing   fleeting
  lasting

082

> A: 오늘 프로젝트 진행이 잘 된 것 같아요.
> B: 동의해요, 저희는 많은 부분을 다루었어요.
> A: 더 마무리해야 할 사항이 있나요?
> B: 제가 생각하기에는 없어요. 모든 것이 제대로 진행되고 있어요.
> A: 좋아요! 그럼, 오늘은 그만합시다.
> B: 좋아요. 내일 뵙겠습니다!

① 사무용품의 배송을 받았나요
② 그것과 관련된 모든 문제를 해결했나요
③ 성과 평가를 마쳤나요

어휘 cover ground (어떤) 부분을 다루다   shipment 배송
office supply 사무용품   resolve 해결하다   performance 성과
finalize 마무리하다

정답 ④

083

해석 그 교육 프로그램은 직원들이 비상사태를 처리할 때 더 자신감 있게 만들도록 설계되었지만, 많은 직원들은 여전히 준비가 안 되었다고 느꼈고 무엇을 해야 할지 확신이 없었다.

어휘 handle 처리하다   emergency 비상사태
unprepared 준비되지 않은   confident 자신감이 있는
hesitant 망설이는   anxious 불안해하는   reluctant 꺼리는

근거

> The training program was designed to make employees more confident in handling emergencies, but many still felt unprepared and unsure of what to do.

정답 ①

주요 어휘 정리

anxious 긴장한   reluctant 꺼리는, 주저하는
= nervous   = hesitant
  apprehensive   unwilling
  worried

084 밑줄 친 부분에 들어갈 말로 가장 적절한 것은?

Sophia Rodriguez
Hey, Steve! Have you heard about David?
10:42

Steve Thompson
No, what happened?
10:43

Sophia Rodriguez
He got food poisoning and had to be hospitalized.
10:44

Steve Thompson
Oh no, poor David! _____.
10:45

Sophia Rodriguez
I was thinking the same thing. Maybe some flowers and a get-well card?
10:46

Steve Thompson
That sounds perfect.
10:47

Sophia Rodriguez
Let's meet at the hospital at 4 PM.
10:48

① Hot weather caused my lunch to go bad
② We should bring him something to cheer him up
③ I had no idea which hospital he was admitted to
④ I've had food poisoning before, just like him

085 밑줄 친 부분에 들어갈 말로 가장 적절한 것은?

The hotel offered _____ breakfast for guests staying in their deluxe suites, allowing them to start their day with a delicious meal at no extra cost.

① spontaneous   ② artificial
③ complimentary   ④ excessive

084

① 날씨가 더워서 내 점심이 상했어
③ 그가 어느 병원에 입원했는지 몰랐어
④ 딱 그처럼 나도 예전에 식중독에 걸렸었어

어휘 food poisoning 식중독 hospitalize 입원시키다
get-well card 쾌유 기원 카드 go bad 상하다
cheer up ~의 기운을 북돋아주다 admit 입원시키다

정답 ②

085

해석 호텔은 디럭스 스위트룸에 투숙하는 투숙객들을 위해 무료 조식을 제공해 추가 비용 없이 맛있는 식사로 하루를 시작할 수 있도록 했다.

어휘 guest 투숙객 deluxe suite 디럭스 스위트룸 extra 추가의
cost 비용 spontaneous 즉흥적인 artificial 인위적인
complimentary 무료의 excessive 과도한

근거

The hotel offered complimentary breakfast for guests staying in their deluxe suites, allowing them to start their day with a delicious meal at no extra cost.

정답 ③

주요 어휘 정리

spontaneous 즉흥적인   complimentary 무료의
= impromtu   = free
  unplanned
  unrehearsed
  improvised
  ad-lib

086 밑줄 친 부분에 들어갈 말로 가장 적절한 것은?

Julia Bennett
Hi, I need help. The taxi came so late that I missed my flight to Rome.
10:42

Airline Staff
Oh no, I'm sorry to hear that. May I have your booking reference number?
10:43

Julia Bennett
Sure, it's #R123456. Is there any way I can get another flight today?
10:44

Airline Staff
There's another flight to Rome in three hours. I can book you on that one, but there may be a rebooking fee.
10:45

Julia Bennett
_____
10:46

Airline Staff
Understood! I'll process your new ticket now. You should receive a confirmation email shortly.
10:48

① Can I get a refund instead?
② How long is the layover?
③ I'd rather wait for tomorrow's flight.
④ I just need to get there as soon as possible.

087 밑줄 친 부분에 들어갈 말로 가장 적절한 것은?

A: Hi, do you have any new shoes in stock?
B: Yes, we just received a new collection of running shoes this week.
A: Great! Do you have them in size 8?
B: Yes, we have size 8 available. Would you like to try them on?
A: Yes, please. _____?
B: No, they don't. Unfortunately, they are only available in white and gray.

① Do you have them in black
② How many color options are available
③ Can I return these next week
④ Are you open on Sundays

086

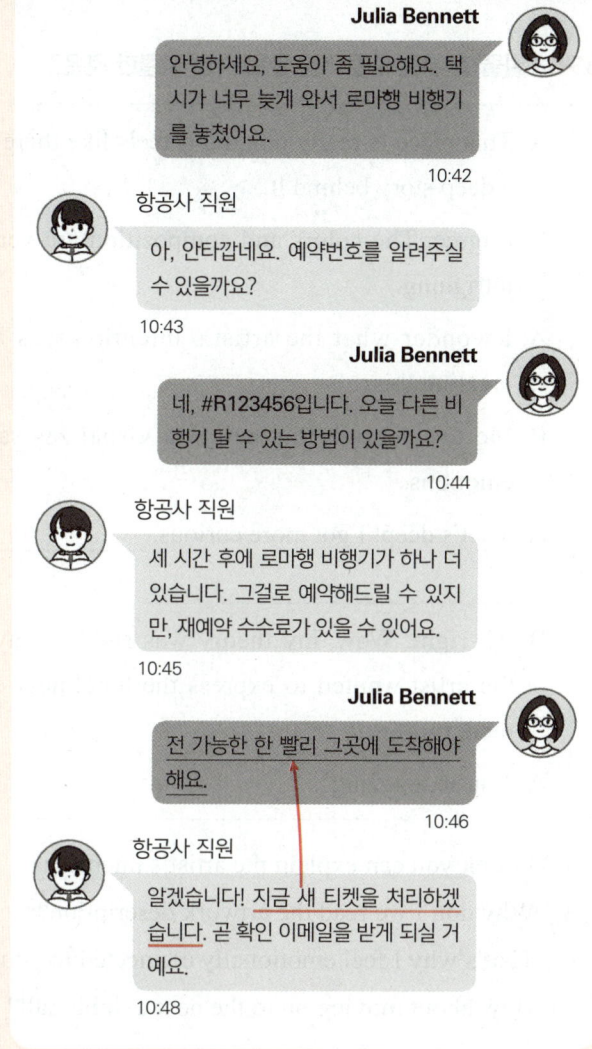

① 대신 환불받을 수 있을까요?
② 경유 시간은 얼마나 되나요?
③ 차라리 내일 비행기를 기다릴게요.

어휘 miss 놓치다 airline 항공사
booking reference number 예약번호 book 예약하다
rebooking 재예약 fee 수수료 Understood! 알겠습니다!
process 처리하다 confirmation 확인 shortly 곧
refund 환불 layover 경유

정답 ④

087

A: 안녕하세요. 새로운 신발이 재고로 있나요?
B: 있습니다. 이번 주에 새로운 운동화 묶음을 받았습니다.
A: 좋군요! 8 사이즈가 있나요?
B: 예, 8 사이즈가 있습니다. 한번 신어보시겠어요?
A: 예 그러죠. 검정색으로 있나요?
B: 아니오. 없습니다. 불행히도 흰색과 회색만 가능합니다.

② 얼마나 다양한 색이 구비되어 있나요
③ 다음 주에 반환해도 될까요
④ 일요일에도 여나요

어휘 in stock 재고로 try on 신어 보다

정답 ①

088 밑줄 친 부분에 들어갈 말로 가장 적절한 것은?

One of the hardest conversations you might have at work is one where you have to _____ your word — you can't meet a deadline, you can't help out with a project, you're unable to reach your quarterly goal, and so on.

① keep
② desert
③ continue
④ break

089 밑줄 친 부분에 들어갈 말로 가장 적절한 것은?

The path to the summit is _____, which requires climbers to use ropes and harnesses.

① sheer
② plain
③ expensive
④ steep

090 밑줄 친 부분에 들어갈 말로 가장 적절한 것은?

A: This piece is really unique. It feels like there's a deep story behind it.
B: I agree. The colors and composition are very intriguing.
A: I wonder what the artist's intention was in creating this.
B: Me too. I think this painting visualizes sad emotions.
A: That's deep. I got more curious. _____ _____
B: All right. Wow, my theory was right. It says the artist wanted to express the loneliness of modern life.
A: You're amazing!

① I think you can explain the artist's intentions.
② Why don't we read the artwork description?
③ That's why I feel emotionally connected to you.
④ How about moving on to the next exhibit hall?

088

해석 직장에서 가장 하기 어려운 대화 중 하나는 약속을 어겨야 하는 대화이다 — 마감일을 맞출 수 없다거나, 프로젝트를 도울 수 없다거나, 분기별 목표를 달성할 수 없다 등등.

어휘 meet a deadline 마감일을 지키다   help out with ~을 돕다
reach 달성하다   quarterly 분기별의   keep 지키다
desert 버리다   continue 계속하다   break 어기다

근거

> One of the hardest conversations you might have at work is one where you have to break your word — you can't meet a deadline, you can't help out with a project, you're unable to reach your quarterly goal, and so on.

정답 ④

주요 어휘 정리
break one's word 약속을 어기다
keep one's word 약속을 지키다

089

해석 산꼭대기로 가는 길은 가팔라서, 등반가들이 로프와 장비를 사용해야 한다.

어휘 summit 산꼭대기   climber 등반가   harness 장비
sheer 순진한   plain 쉬운   expensive 비싼   steep 가파른

근거

> The path to the summit is steep, which requires climbers to use ropes and harnesses.

정답 ④

주요 어휘 정리
sheer 순전한   plain 쉬운, 평이한
= total   = simple
  absolute   easy
  utter

090

> A: 이 작품 정말 독특하네요. 이면에 심오한 이야기가 담겨 있는 것 같아요.
> B: 동의해요. 색감과 구도가 아주 흥미로워요.
> A: 작가가 어떤 의도로 이 작품을 만들었는지 궁금해지네요.
> B: 저도요. 이 그림은 슬픈 감정을 시각화한 것 같아요.
> A: 심오하네요. 더 궁금해졌어요. 작품 해설을 읽어보는 게 어때요?
> B: 좋아요. 와, 제 생각이 맞았어요. 화가가 현대 생활의 외로움을 표현하려 했다고 쓰여 있어요.
> A: 정말 대단하세요!

① 당신이 화가의 의도를 설명해줄 수 있을 것 같아요.
③ 그런 이유로 저는 정서적으로 당신과 연결된 기분이에요.
④ 다음 전시실로 넘어가는 게 어때요?

어휘 piece 작품   unique 독특한   composition 구도
intriguing 아주 흥미로운   intention 의도   visualize 시각화하다
emotion 감정   curious 궁금한   theory 생각
loneliness 외로움   description 해설   move on to ~로 넘어가다
exhibit hall 전시실

정답 ②

091 밑줄 친 부분에 들어갈 말로 가장 적절한 것은?

> If a person is described as _____, this means that they do not trust other people easily and are often suspicious of their motives.

① naive ② outgoing
③ skeptical ④ generous

092 밑줄 친 부분에 들어갈 말로 가장 적절한 것은?

> A: Hello, I want to check out. Here is my room key.
> B: Just one second, sir, and I'll give you your receipt. Here you go.
> A: Thank you very much.
> B: Sir, how did you enjoy your stay at New York Hotel?
> A: _____, but my time in New York was thoroughly delightful.
> B: I apologize for any inconvenience caused during your stay. I assure you that we will offer a clean, bug-free room next time.

① I haven't received my receipt yet
② I found the hotel facilities to be satisfactory
③ I appreciated the helpfulness of the hotel staff
④ I wish there had been no insects in the hotel

093 밑줄 친 빈칸에 들어갈 말로 가장 적절한 것은?

 Emma Garcia
Hey Jake, have you had a chance to look at the project brief?
10:42

 Jake Wilson
Yeah, I read through it this morning. There's a lot to cover, especially the timeline section.
10:43

 Emma Garcia
Agreed. I'm working on the agenda now. By the way, do you think you could prepare a short summary of the main reports?
10:44

 Jake Wilson
Sure, I can do that. When do you need it by?
10:45

 Emma Garcia
Ideally by Friday afternoon. That way we'll have the weekend to make any changes.
10:46

 Jake Wilson
Sounds good. _____.
10:48

 Emma Garcia
Perfect. Thanks!
10:49

① I'll try to send it sometime next week if I have time
② I'll get started on it today and send it over by tomorrow or Friday morning
③ I haven't even read the brief yet, to be honest
④ I think the reports aren't important for this meeting

문장 분석 및 해설

091

해석 어떤 사람이 회의적이라고 묘사된다면, 이는 그 사람이 다른 사람을 쉽게 믿지 않으며 그들의 동기를 종종 의심한다는 뜻이다.

어휘 describe 묘사하다 suspicious 의심하는 motive 동기
naive 순진한 outgoing 외향적인 skeptical 회의적인
generous 관대한

근거
> If a person is described as skeptical, this means that they do not trust other people easily and are often suspicious of their motives.

정답 ③

주요 어휘 정리

naive 순진한
= ingenuous

outgoing 사교적인
= sociable
  social
  gregarious

skeptical 회의적인
= doubtful
  suspicious
  incredulous

generous 관대한
= lenient
  permissive
  indulgent

092

> A: 안녕하세요, 체크아웃하려고 합니다. 여기 제 방 열쇠입니다.
> B: 잠시만 기다려 주세요, 손님. 영수증 드리겠습니다. 여기 있습니다.
> A: 정말 감사합니다.
> B: 손님, 뉴욕 호텔에서의 숙박은 어땠나요?
> A: 호텔에 벌레가 없었더라면 좋았을 테지만, 뉴욕에서의 시간은 대단히 즐거웠어요.
> B: 숙박 중 불편을 드려 죄송합니다. 다음번에는 벌레 없는, 깨끗한 객실을 제공하겠다고 약속드립니다.

① 아직 영수증을 받지 못했지만
② 호텔 시설이 만족스러웠지만
③ 호텔 직원들의 친절에 감사했지만

어휘 receipt 영수증 stay 숙박 thoroughly 대단히
delightful 즐거운 inconvenience 불편 facility 시설
satisfactory 만족스러운

정답 ④

093

① 시간 나면 다음 주 언젠가 보내볼게
③ 솔직하게 말하면 난 개요서를 아직 읽지도 않았어
④ 그 보고서는 이번 회의에 중요하지 않다고 생각해

어휘 brief 개요서 cover 다루다 timeline 일정 agenda 안건
report 보고서 to be honest 솔직히

정답 ②

094 밑줄 친 부분에 들어갈 말로 가장 적절한 것은?

> A: Did you catch that documentary everyone's talking about?
> B: Yeah, it was eye-opening.
> A: What struck you the most about the documentary?
> B: The visuals of melting ice caps were powerful.
> A: Right, the impact of climate change is a critical issue.
> B: _____.
> A: There are plenty of people just like you. So, it's important to promote global warming to the public.

① I hadn't realized how important it was until I saw that
② I usually watch documentaries whenever I have time
③ After watching that, a happy thought struck me
④ I always put weight on promoting environmental issues

095 밑줄 친 부분에 들어갈 말로 가장 적절한 것은?

> If someone is described as _____, it means they remain calm and focused even when facing intense pressure or unexpected challenges.

① anxious   ② composed
③ reckless   ④ irritable

096 밑줄 친 부분에 들어갈 말로 가장 적절한 것은?

 Soojin: Hey, did you manage to book the restaurant for Friday's team dinner? 10:42

 Jiwon: Yes, I made a reservation for 7 p.m. at Bella Italia. It's confirmed for 8 people. 10:43

 Soojin: Perfect, thanks for handling that! 10:44

 Jiwon: No problem. _____ _____? 10:45

 Soojin: Yes, I already told everyone about the time but not the place. I'll let them know the place soon. 10:46

 Jiwon: Great. Looking forward to it! 10:47

① Did you check if the restaurant has vegetarian options
② Did you inform the team about the reservation details
③ Should we change the number of people for the reservation
④ Do you think we should book a room at another restaurant

094

> A: 모두가 이야기하는 그 다큐멘터리 봤어?
> B: 눈이 번쩍 뜨이게 하는 거였어.
> A: 다큐멘터리에서 무엇이 가장 강한 인상을 주었어?
> B: 녹아내리는 만년설의 영상이 강렬했어.
> A: 그래, 기후변화의 영향은 아주 중요한 문제야.
> B: 그 다큐멘터리를 보기 전까지는 그게 얼마나 중요한지 몰랐어.
> A: 너 같은 사람들이 많아. 그래서, 지구 온난화를 대중에게 널리 알리는 게 중요한 거야.

② 나는 시간이 날 때마다 대개 다큐멘터리를 봐
③ 그걸 시청한 뒤에, 행복한 생각이 떠올랐어
④ 나는 환경 문제를 널리 알리는 것을 항상 중요하게 여겨

어휘 catch (방송 등을) 보다   eye-opening 눈이 번쩍 뜨이게 하는
strike 강한 인상을 주다, 떠오르다   ice cap 만년설   impact 영향
plenty of 많은   promote 널리 알리다   realize 깨닫다
put weight on ~을 중요하게 여기다   environmental 환경의

정답 ①

095

해석 어떤 사람이 평정을 유지한다고 묘사된다면, 그것은 극심한 압박이나 예상치 못한 도전에 직면할 때조차도 그 사람이 침착하고 집중력을 유지한다는 의미이다.

어휘 remain (~ 상태를) 유지하다   calm 침착한   focused 집중하는
face 직면하다   intense 극심한   pressure 압박
unexpected 예상치 못한   challenge 도전   anxious 불안해하는
composed 평정을 유지하는   reckless 무모한
irritable 짜증을 잘 내는

근거

> If someone is described as <u>composed</u>, it means they <u>remain calm and focused</u> even when facing intense pressure or unexpected challenges.

정답 ②

주요 어휘 정리

anxious 긴장한	reckless 부주의한
= nervous	= careless
apprehensive	heedless
worried	

096

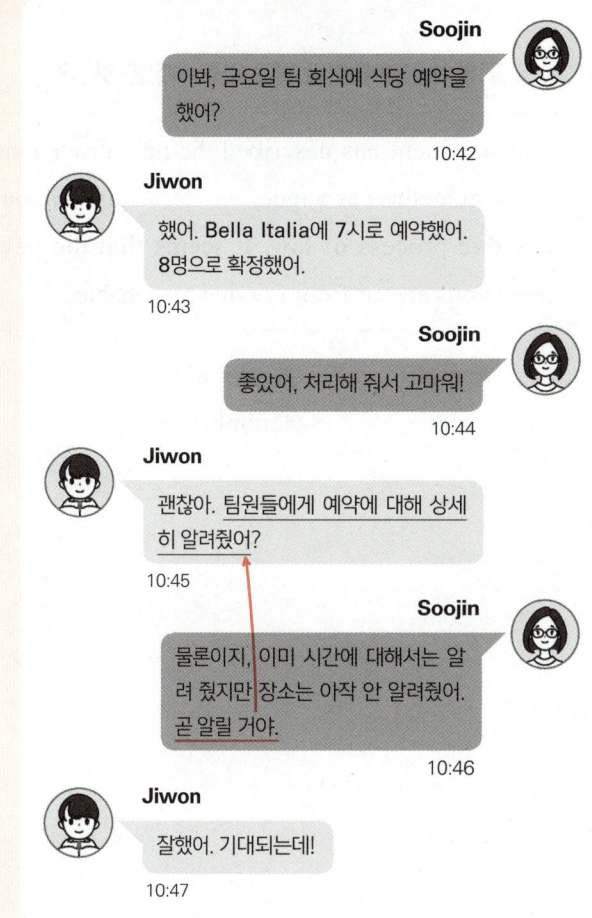

① 식당이 채식주의자에 대한 선택지가 있는지 확인했어
③ 예약인 수를 바꿔야 할까
④ 다른 식당에 방을 예약해야 한다고 생각해

어휘 book 예약하다   team dinner 팀 회식
make a reservation 예약하다   confirm 확인하다
handle 처리하다   vegetarian 채식주의자

정답 ②

097 밑줄 친 부분에 들어갈 말로 가장 적절한 것은?

> The statement has described the new provisions in the guidelines as vague, _____ and without any due process of law. It seems that the new provisions are far from fair and reasonable.

① incessant ② arbitrary
③ incurable ④ nimble

098 밑줄 친 부분에 들어갈 말로 가장 적절한 것은?

Carlos Walker
Lisa, are you ready for the client presentation this afternoon?
10:42

 Lisa Lee
Almost. Just finalizing a few slides. What time is the meeting?
10:43

Carlos Walker
It's at 2 PM.
10:44

 Lisa Lee
Hmm... are you swamped with work now?
10:45

Carlos Walker
No, I'm pretty open at this point.
10:46

 Lisa Lee
I'm wondering _____ _____.
10:47

Carlos Walker
Sure, send them over. I'll check them right away.
10:48

 Lisa Lee
Thanks, Carlos. I appreciate it!
10:49

① if you gave the client presentation
② if there's too much to catch up on
③ if you will attend the meeting or not
④ if you can review the big data slides

097

해석 그 성명서는 지침의 새로운 조항들이 막연하고, 자의적이고, 정당한 법 절차가 전혀 없다고 설명했다. 새로운 조항은 공정하고 합리적인 것과는 거리가 먼 것 같다.

어휘 statement 성명(서) provision 조항 guideline 지침
vague 모호한 due process of law 정당한 법 절차
incessant 끊임없는 arbitrary 자의적인 incurable 불치의
nimble 기민한

근거

> The statement has described the new provisions in the guidelines as vague, arbitrary and without any due process of law. It seems that the new provisions are far from fair and reasonable.

정답 ②

주요 어휘 정리

incessant 끊임없는
= constant
  unceasing
  ceaseless
  permanent
  persistent

arbitrary 자의적인
= random
  unplanned

incurable 불치의
= untreatable
  irremediable
  beyond cure
  terminal

nimble 기민한
= shrewd
  astute
  agile
  canny
  speedy
  quick

098

① 당신이 고객 프레젠테이션을 했나
② 따라잡아야 할 일이 많은가
③ 당신이 회의에 참석할 건가

어휘 finalize 마무리하다 swamped 무척 바쁜 open 한가한
catch up on ~을 따라잡다

정답 ④

099 밑줄 친 부분에 들어갈 말로 가장 적절한 것은?

> The tears began to fall faster as Paul couldn't _____ his emotions.

① postpone
② withhold
③ cause
④ hinder

100 밑줄 친 부분에 들어갈 말로 가장 적절한 것은?

 Emily Chen
Can you believe we're about to graduate?
10:42

 Ryan Kim
I know, it's unbelievable! Congrats!
10:43

 Emily Chen
Thanks! Same to you!
10:44

 Ryan Kim
By the way, I wonder _____ _____.
10:45

 Emily Chen
According to the schedule, about two hours.
10:46

 Ryan Kim
I'm going to cherish every minute of it.
10:47

 Emily Chen
That's the way to go!
10:49

① when we can receive our diplomas
② how long the commencement is going to be
③ what your plans are after this
④ how long it took you to graduate

099

[해석] Paul이 감정을 억제하지 못하자 눈물이 더 빨리 떨어지기 시작했다.

[어휘] tears 눈물   emotion 감정   postpone 미루다
withhold 억제하다   cause 일으키다   hinder 방해하다

[근거]
> The tears began to fall faster as Paul couldn't withhold his emotions.

[정답] ②

[주요 어휘 정리]

postpone 미루다
= delay
  suspend
  defer
  put off
  hold off

withhold 억제하다
= control
  check
  hold back

cause 일으키다
= generate
  produce
  create
  bring about
  give rise to
  touch off

hinder 방해하다
= impede
  deter
  thwart
  hamper
  disturb
  interrupt
  set back

100

① 언제 우리가 졸업장을 받을지
③ 이 이후에 너의 계획이 무엇인지
④ 네가 졸업하는 데 얼마나 걸렸는지

[어휘] graduate 졸업하다   unbelievable 믿을 수 없는
by the way 그런데   cherish 소중히 여기다   diploma 졸업장
commencement 학위 수여식

[정답] ②

101 밑줄 친 부분에 들어갈 말로 가장 적절한 것은?

Sarah Stewart
Dad, I'm at the test center, but there's a problem.
10:42

Dad
What's wrong?
10:43

Sarah Stewart
I forgot to bring my ID.
10:44

Dad
Can't you use your student ID?
10:45

Sarah Stewart
I lost it at school last month.
10:46

Dad
Did you ask the staff what to do?
10:47

Sarah Stewart
_____.
10:48

Dad
Got it. I'll bring it right away.
10:49

① They said my passport would do
② They found my ID at the library
③ They said the test center has moved
④ They said I can't take the test

102 밑줄 친 부분에 들어갈 말로 가장 적절한 것은?

Despite numerous attempts to change his mind, he remained _____ and refused to listen to any alternative opinions.

① humble   ② obstinate
③ diligent   ④ intellectual

101

① 직원들이 내 신분증을 도서관에서 찾았대요
② 직원들이 이 시험장이 이전됐다고 했어요
③ 직원들이 제가 시험을 볼 수 없다고 했어요

어휘 student ID 학생증   passport 여권   do 괜찮다

정답 ①

102

해석 그의 마음을 바꾸려는 수많은 시도에도 불구하고, 그는 여전히 고집이 셌고, 어떤 대안적인 의견도 듣기를 거부했다.

어휘 numerous 수많은   attempt 시도   refuse 거부하다
alternative 대안적인   humble 겸손한   obstinate 고집 센
diligent 부지런한   intellectual 지적인

근거
> Despite numerous attempts to change his mind, he remained obstinate and refused to listen to any alternative opinions.

정답 ②

주요 어휘 정리
obstinate 고집 센
= stubborn
  inflexible
  intractable
  unadaptable
  headstrong

103 밑줄 친 부분에 들어갈 말로 가장 적절한 것은?

> When the internet connection kept dropping during his important video call, the boss became _____ and started complaining loudly.

① grateful ② irritated
③ amused   ④ relieved

104 밑줄 친 부분에 들어갈 말로 가장 적절한 것은?

Amy Brooks
Hey, I'm moving into my new apartment tomorrow. Could you lend me a hand with moving stuff?
10:42

Liam Foster
Sure thing! What are neighbors for?
10:43

Amy Brooks
Thanks a lot! Can you come over around noon?
10:44

Liam Foster
No problem. Should I bring any tools or just my muscles?
10:45

Amy Brooks
Actually, _____.
10:46

Liam Foster
I see. I'll bring my tool box with me.
10:48

① I can buy tools in a nearby store
② movers will take care of it
③ just your muscles should do
④ I need to drive some screws

103

[해석] 인터넷 연결이 중요한 화상 통화 중에 계속 끊기자, 사장님은 화가 나서 큰 소리로 불평하기 시작했다.

[어휘] complain 불평하다　loudly 큰 소리로　grateful 감사하는　irritated 화가 난　amused 기쁜　relieved 안심한

[근거]

> When the internet connection kept dropping during his important video call, the boss became irritated and started complaining loudly.

[정답] ②

[주요 어휘 정리]
irritated 화가 난
= furious
　indignant
　angry
　infuriated
　enraged

104

① 내가 근처 가게에서 공구를 살 수 있을거야
② 이사꾼들이 해결할 거야
③ 그냥 몸만 와도 충분해

[어휘] lend a hand 도와주다　Sure thing. 물론.
What are neighbors for? 이웃 좋다는 게 뭐야?　nearby 근처의
do 되다[충분하다]

[정답] ④

105 밑줄 친 부분에 들어갈 말로 가장 적절한 것은?

> There are many kinds of businesses and they sell various things. If they suffer a loss in one division, they can _____ for it with a gain in another division.

① search　　② account
③ apply　　　④ compensate

106 밑줄 친 부분에 들어갈 말로 가장 적절한 것은?

> The doctor was able to _____ the patient's condition and propose a treatment plan after conducting several tests.

① wound　　② diagnose
③ bend　　　④ bruise

107 밑줄 친 부분에 들어갈 말로 가장 적절한 것은?

> A: Did you see the revised layout for the lobby?
> B: Not yet. Where can I check it?
> A: It's in the email from the interior team.
> B: I must have missed that.
> A: They added a new reception desk design.
> B: I see. I'll take a look now.
> A: Oh, _____
> B: Got it. I'll focus on that area first.

① the email has been deleted already.
② will the front desk be closed until Monday?
③ pay attention to the layout near the front.
④ don't you need to check emails anymore?

105

해석 다양한 사업체가 있고, 그들은 다양한 것을 판다. 그들은 한 사업부에서 손해를 보면 다른 사업부에서의 이익으로 그것을 만회할 수 있다.

어휘 suffer a loss 손해를 보다   division 부(部)   gain 이익
search for ~을 찾다   account for ~을 설명하다
apply for ~을 신청[지원]하다   compensate for ~을 만회하다

근거

> There are many kinds of businesses. They sell various things. If they suffer a loss in one division, they can compensate for it with a gain in another division.

정답 ④

주요 어휘 정리
compensate for ~을 만회하다
= make up for
　offset

106

해석 의사는 여러 차례 검사를 실시한 후에 환자의 상태를 진단하고 치료 계획을 제안할 수 있었다.

어휘 patient 환자   condition 상태   treatment 치료
conduct 실시하다   wound 부상을 입히다   diagnose 진단하다
bend 구부리다   bruise 타박상을 입히다

근거

> The doctor was able to diagnose the patient's condition and propose a treatment plan after conducting several tests.

정답 ②

주요 어휘 정리
wound 부상을 입히다
= hurt
　injure

diagnose 진단하다
= identify
　determine
　detect

107

> A: 로비의 수정된 배치도 봤어?
> B: 아직 못 봤어. 어디서 확인할 수 있어?
> A: 인테리어 팀에서 보낸 이메일에 있어.
> B: 내가 그걸 놓쳤나 봐.
> A: 새 안내 데스크 디자인을 추가했더라.
> B: 그렇구나. 지금 확인해볼게.
> A: 오, 건물 앞쪽 근처의 배치도를 신경 써서 봐.
> B: 알겠어. 그 부분부터 집중해서 볼게.

① 이메일이 이미 지워졌네.
② 안내 데스크가 월요일까지 닫는 거야?
④ 이메일은 이제 볼 필요가 없지 않아?

어휘 revise 수정하다   layout 배치도   entrance 입구

정답 ③

108 밑줄 친 부분에 들어갈 말로 가장 적절한 것은?

> Experts say, to be truly _____, you need to be actively prepared for change and be consistently developing more skills in order to meet emerging needs.

① adaptable
② lucrative
③ arrogant
④ mandatory

109 밑줄 친 부분에 들어갈 말로 가장 적절한 것은?

> A: We should start preparing dinner soon.
> B: Okay, I'll help chop the vegetables.
> A: Thanks. Could you also set the table?
> B: What's the rush? Dinner isn't for another hour.
> A: _____
> B: You're thoroughly prepared. Okay, I'll do it now.
> A: Perfect. Thanks a lot!

① We will just order takeout instead.
② I just want everything ready before guests arrive.
③ I think we should wait until the guests arrive.
④ Let's do everything last minute to keep it exciting.

110 밑줄 친 부분에 들어갈 말로 가장 적절한 것은?

> A: Have you experienced any unusual symptoms lately?
> B: Yes, I've been sneezing a lot and my eyes are itching.
> A: Have you eaten anything different recently that could trigger allergies?
> B: Hmm... I don't think so.
> A: It's important to recall any changes in your diet or environment.
> B: Actually, now that you mention it, _____ _____.
> A: Ah, that could be the trigger. Let's consider allergy testing to confirm.

① I haven't noticed any changes recently
② I did try a new type of nut last week
③ allergies can be triggered by various causes
④ I haven't eaten anything in a while

108

해석 전문가들은 진정으로 (새로운 환경에) 적응할 수 있으려면, 적극적으로 변화에 준비되어 있어야 하고 새로운 요구를 충족시킬 수 있도록 더 많은 기술을 지속적으로 개발해야 한다고 말한다.

어휘 consistently 지속적으로　emerging 새로운
adaptable 적응할 수 있는　lucrative 수익성이 좋은
arrogant 거만한　mandatory 의무적인

근거
> Experts say, to be truly adaptable, you need to be actively prepared for change and be consistently developing more skills in order to meet emerging needs.

정답 ①

주요 어휘 정리

adaptable 적응할 수 있는
= flexible
　resilient
　adjustable

lucrative 수익성이 좋은
= profitable
　money-making
　gainful

arrogant 거만한
= haughty
　supercilious
　pompous
　stuck-up

mandatory 의무적인
= compulsory
　obligatory
　requisite
　forced
　required

109

> A: 우리 곧 저녁 준비를 시작해야 해.
> B: 알겠어, 내가 채소 써는 것을 도울게.
> A: 고마워. 상도 차려줄 수 있어?
> B: 왜 이렇게 서둘러? 저녁까지 아직 한 시간 정도 남았잖아.
> A: 난 그냥 손님들이 오기 전에 모든 걸 준비해 놓고 싶어.
> B: 넌 준비성이 철저하구나. 좋아, 지금 차릴게.
> A: 완벽해. 정말 고마워!

① 대신 그냥 배달로 주문할거야.
③ 손님들이 도착할 때까지 기다려야 할 것 같아.
④ 계속 신나도록 막판에 모든 걸 다 하자.

어휘 prepare 준비하다　chop 썰다　set the table 상을 차리다
What's the rush? 왜 이렇게 서둘러?　thoroughly 철저히
last minute 막판에

정답 ②

110

> A: 최근에 특이한 증상을 겪지 않았나요?
> B: 네, 재채기를 많이 하고 눈이 가려워요.
> A: 최근에 알레르기를 유발할 만한 색다른 것을 드셨나요?
> B: 음... 그랬던 것 같지 않아요.
> A: 식단이나 환경에 생긴 어떤 변화라도 기억하는 게 중요해요.
> B: 실은, 그 말을 듣고 보니, 지난주에 새로운 종류의 견과류를 먹어 봤어요.
> A: 아, 그게 계기일 수도 있겠네요. 확인해보게 알레르기 검사를 고려해 봅시다.

① 최근에 어떤 변화도 알아차리지 못했어요
③ 알레르기는 다양한 원인으로 유발될 수 있어요
④ 한동안 아무것도 먹지 않았어요

어휘 unusual 특이한　symptom 증상　sneeze 재채기하다
itching 가려운　trigger 유발하다; 계기　recall 기억하다
now that you mention it 그 말을 듣고 보니　confirm 확인하다
notice 알아차리다

정답 ②

111 밑줄 친 부분에 들어갈 말로 가장 적절한 것은?

Lily Harris
How did you like the independent film I recommended?
10:42

Brian Nelson
I really enjoyed it! The story was so refreshing. I've never seen anything like it before.
10:43

Lily Harris
The director always tries new and creative things.
10:44

Brian Nelson
He created remarkable scenes using impressive color and sound effects.
10:45

Lily Harris
You are right. And the director is famous for creating unique characters.
10:46

Brian Nelson
Oh, _____?
10:47

Lily Harris
Then, I'll give you a list of his best films.
10:48

① would you like go to see blockbusters together
② can you recommend his other movies to watch
③ is that why you prefer watching popular movies
④ do you think his movies was a total disaster

112 밑줄 친 부분에 들어갈 말로 가장 적절한 것은?

According to research, social media is being used around the world to _____ public opinion by governments and individuals through the promotion of lies, misinformation, and propaganda.

① supplant
② elucidate
③ condense
④ manipulate

113 밑줄 친 부분에 들어갈 말로 가장 적절한 것은?

A: I can't believe the discounted price of this sweater. I think it's a good bargain.
B: But you can only get the discount if you have the coupon downloaded through the website.
A: Oh, I see. All I need to do is to go to the website and download a coupon?
B: That's right. But to download the coupon, you need to sign up as a member first.
A: I got it. _____
B: Sure. Let me show you how to sign up.

① I'll just look for another store instead.
② That sounds too complicated. I'll pass.
③ Can I do that right now on my smartphone?
④ Can you show me the way to the information desk?

문장 분석 및 해설

111

Lily Harris: 제가 추천해 드린 독립영화는 어떠셨나요? 10:42

Brian Nelson: 정말 재미있었어요! 이야기가 정말 신선했어요. 이런 건 전에 본 적이 없어요. 10:43

Lily Harris: 그 감독은 항상 새롭고 창조적인 것들을 시도해요. 10:44

Brian Nelson: 그는 인상적인 색채와 음향 효과를 사용하여 주목할 만한 장면을 만들어냈어요. 10:45

Lily Harris: 맞아요. 그리고 그 감독은 독특한 캐릭터를 만드는 것으로 유명해요. 10:46

Brian Nelson: 오, 볼 만한 그의 다른 영화를 추천해 줄 수 있나요? 10:47

Lily Harris: 그렇다면, 그의 걸작 목록을 드릴게요. 10:48

① 블록버스터 영화를 같이 보러 갈래요
③ 그런 이유로 인기 영화 보는 걸 좋아하시나요
④ 그의 영화가 완전히 실패작이라고 생각하세요

어휘 independent 독립의 film 영화 recommend 추천하다
refreshing 신선한 director 감독 creative 창의적인
remarkable 주목할 만한 scene 장면 impressive 인상적인
sound effect 음향 효과 prefer 선호하다 disaster 실패작

정답 ②

112

해석 연구에 따르면, 소셜 미디어는 전 세계적으로 정부와 개인들에 의해 거짓, 잘못된 정보, 그리고 선전의 유포를 통해 여론을 조작하는 데 사용되고 있다.

어휘 public opinion 여론 misinformation 잘못된 정보
propaganda (허위·과장된 정치) 선전 supplant 대신하다
elucidate 설명하다 condense 압축하다 manipulate 조작하다

근거

> According to research, social media is being used around the world to <u>manipulate</u> public opinion by governments and individuals <u>through the promotion of lies, misinformation, and propaganda.</u>

정답 ④

주요 어휘 정리

supplant 대신[대체]하다	condense (글·정보를) 압축하다
= replace	= abridge
supersede	shorten
substitute	
take the place of	

manipulate 조작하다
= control
  exploit

113

A: 이 스웨터의 할인 가격을 믿을 수가 없어요. 특가품 같아요.
B: 하지만 홈페이지를 통해 쿠폰을 다운로드 받아야만 할인을 받으실 수 있어요.
A: 아, 그렇군요. 홈페이지에 들어가서 쿠폰을 다운로드하기만 하면 되나요?
B: 맞습니다. 하지만 <u>쿠폰을 다운로드하려면 회원가입을 먼저 하셔야 해요.</u>
A: 알겠습니다. <u>지금 바로 제 스마트폰으로 해도 되나요?</u>
B: 네. <u>제가 가입하는 법을 알려드릴게요.</u>

① 그냥 다른 가게를 찾아볼게요.
② 그거 너무 복잡하게 들리네요. 전 그냥 안 할게요.
④ 안내 데스크로 가는 길 좀 알려주시겠어요?

어휘 good bargain 특가품 sign up 가입하다 complicated 복잡한

정답 ③

DAY 12

114 밑줄 친 부분에 들어갈 말로 가장 적절한 것은?

> In the Third World, many pirate publishers _____ copyrights by illegally copying copyrighted books from developed countries.

① infringe ② salvage
③ rebel ④ capture

115 밑줄 친 부분에 들어갈 말로 가장 적절한 것은?

> While public sector unions have _____ because the public sector itself has grown, private sector unions have been wiped out by globalization.

① withdrawn ② thrived
③ monopolized ④ vanished

116 밑줄 친 부분에 들어갈 말로 가장 적절한 것은?

> A: Are you managing your blood sugar well these days?
> B: Yes, I'm paying more attention to my diet. I'm especially trying to cut down on carbs.
> A: That's great. Are you exercising regularly?
> B: Yes, I've been walking for 30 minutes every day. It really helps with blood sugar control.
> A: Absolutely, exercise is really important. Are you taking your medication regularly?
> B: _____.
> A: You're doing a good job. Keep it up, and things will keep improving!

① I've been forgetting to take it most days
② I make sure to take it as my doctor prescribed
③ I take it whenever I feel like it
④ You are doing things to boost your immunity

114

해석 제 3세계에서는 많은 해적 출판사들이 선진국의 저작권이 있는 책들을 불법 복제함으로써 저작권을 침해한다.

어휘 pirate 해적의   publisher 출판사   developed country 선진국
infringe 침해하다   salvage 구조하다   rebel 반항하다
capture 사로잡다

근거

> In the Third World, many pirate publishers infringe copyrights by illegally copying copyrighted books from developed countries.

정답 ①

주요 어휘 정리

infringe 침해하다
= violate
  trespass

salvage 구조하다
= save
  rescue

rebel 반항하다
= oppose
  resist
  disobey
  defy

capture 사로잡다
= captivate
  fascinate
  enchant

115

해석 공공부문의 노조는 공공부문 자체가 성장했기 때문에 번창한 반면에, 민간부문 노조는 세계화로 인해 전멸했다.

어휘 sector 부문   union 노조   wipe out 전멸시키다
withdraw 철회하다   thrive 번창하다   monopolize 독점하다
vanish 사라지다

근거

> While public sector unions have thrived because the public sector itself has grown, private sector unions have been wiped out by globalization.

정답 ②

주요 어휘 정리

withdraw 철회하다
= abolish   rescind
  annul   recall
  revoke
  repeal

thrive 번영하다
= flourish
  prosper
  bloom

vanish 사라지다
= disappear   fade away
  perish   pass away
  die

116

A: 요즘 혈당은 잘 관리하고 있어요?

B: 네, 식단에 더 신경 쓰고 있어요. 특히 탄수화물 식품을 줄이려고 노력 중이에요.

A: 잘하고 있네요. 운동은 규칙적으로 하고 있어요?

B: 네, 하루에 30분씩 걷기를 하고 있어요. 혈당 조절에 정말 도움이 돼요.

A: 맞아요, 운동은 정말 중요하죠. 약은 규칙적으로 먹고 있죠?

B: 의사 선생님께서 처방해 주신 대로 꼭 챙겨 먹고 있어요.

A: 잘하고 있어요. 꾸준히 하면, 계속해서 좋아질 거예요!

① 거의 매일 그것을 먹는 것을 까먹고 있어요
③ 제가 먹고 싶을 때마다 먹어요
④ 당신은 면역력을 높이기 위해 여러 가지 일을 하고 있어요

어휘 manage 관리하다   blood sugar 혈당
pay attention to ~에 신경을 쓰다   diet 식단
cut down on ~을 줄이다   carbs 탄수화물 식품
exercise 운동하다   regularly 규칙적으로   control 조절
medication 약   Keep it up. 꾸준히 해요.   most days 거의 매일
prescribe 처방하다   boost 높이다   immunity 면역력

정답 ②

117 밑줄 친 부분에 들어갈 말로 가장 적절한 것은?

> The new restaurant in town offers a diverse menu of delicious dishes at _____ prices, making it a favorite among budget-conscious diners.

① irrational   ② affordable
③ superior   ④ prosperous

118 밑줄 친 부분에 들어갈 말로 가장 적절한 것은?

> A: What can I do for you today?
> B: I have a problem with charges on my debit card.
> A: Do you have a statement for your debit card?
> B: Here you are.
> A: What are the charges you're referring to?
> B: The last four charges on the page.
> A: I'm afraid _____.
> B: How long will that take?
> A: I'm not sure, but in the meantime we will freeze these charges.
> B: That's wonderful. Thank you.

① you have to pay a late fee for these charges
② there's nothing we can do for you
③ we're going to have to investigate these charges
④ you cannot evade paying unknown charges

117

해석 마을의 새로운 식당은 다양한 메뉴의 맛있는 요리를 <u>저렴한</u> 가격에 제공하여, 가격을 중시하는 손님들 사이에 가장 인기 있는 곳이 되었다.

어휘 diverse 다양한   dish 요리   favorite 가장 인기 있는 것[곳]
budget-conscious 가격을 중시하는   diner (식당의) 손님
irrational 비이성적인   affordable 저렴한   superior 우월한
prosperous 번성하는

근거

> The new restaurant in town offers a diverse menu of delicious dishes at <u>affordable</u> prices, making it a favorite among budget-conscious diners.

정답 ②

주요 어휘 정리
affordable 저렴한
= reasonable
　low
　competitive
　budget-friendly
　economical

118

> A: 오늘 무엇을 도와드릴까요?
> B: 제 직불카드에 청구된 요금에 문제가 있습니다.
> A: 직불카드에 대한 명세서가 있나요?
> B: 여기 있습니다.
> A: 어떤 요금을 말씀하시는 건가요?
> B: 그 페이지의 마지막 네 가지 요금입니다.
> A: 죄송하지만 <u>이 요금들에 대해 조사를 해야 할 것 같습니다</u>.
> B: 얼마나 걸릴까요?
> A: 확실하지 않습니다, 그러나 그 사이에 이 요금을 동결할 것입니다.
> B: 잘됐네요. 감사합니다.

① 이 요금들에 대한 연체료를 지불해야 합니다
② 저희가 할 수 있는 게 없습니다
④ 알 수 없는 요금을 내는 것을 피할 수 없습니다

어휘 charge 요금   debit card 직불카드   statement 명세서
in the meantime 그 사이에   freeze 동결하다   a late fee 연체료
investigate 조사하다   evade 피하다

정답 ③

119 밑줄 친 부분에 들어갈 말로 가장 적절한 것은?

> Many smaller businesses have become _____ because of economic stagnation.

① insolvent ② prosperous
③ lively   ④ optimistic

120 밑줄 친 부분에 들어갈 말로 가장 적절한 것은?

Sarah Johnson
Hello, I'm interested in booking a room at your hotel for a weekend getaway.
10:42

 Aloa Hotel
Hi, Sarah! We'd be delighted to assist you. How many nights will you be staying?
10:43

Sarah Johnson
We plan to stay for two nights, from Friday to Sunday.
10:44

 Aloa Hotel
Great! Would you like to book a standard room?
10:45

Sarah Johnson
_____.
10:46

 Aloa Hotel
We have several suites available for those dates. They offer more space and luxury, though a little bit expensive.
10:47

Sarah Johnson
That would be wonderful. I'll take one of those.
10:48

① Yes, it's ideal for our visit's purpose
② We're looking for something cheaper
③ No, we're interested in an upgrade
④ I'm satisfied with a range of amenities

119

[해석] 많은 영세사업자들이 경제 침체로 인해 파산했다.

[어휘] stagnation 침체 insolvent 파산한 prosperous 번영한
lively 생기 넘치는 optimistic 낙관적인

[근거]
> Many smaller businesses have become insolvent because of economic stagnation.

[정답] ①

[주요 어휘 정리]

insolvent 파산한
= bankrupt
  broke

prosperous 번영한, 번창한
= flourishing
  thriving
  successful

120

① 네, 그 방이 우리 방문 목적에 잘 맞아요
② 우리는 더 저렴한 것을 찾고 있어요
④ 다양한 설비에 만족하고 있어요

[어휘] book 예약하다 getaway 휴가 available 이용 가능한
luxury 호화로움 expensive 비싼 purpose 목적
amenities (pl.) 설비

[정답] ③

121. 밑줄 친 부분에 들어갈 말로 가장 적절한 것은?

> She decided to _____ from voting on the controversial proposal to avoid influencing the outcome unfairly.

① recover   ② investigate
③ rescue   ④ abstain

122. 밑줄 친 부분에 들어갈 말로 가장 적절한 것은?

> A: Oh no! I have a loose tooth.
> B: Seriously? You should go see a dentist before it's too late.
> A: No. I will just leave it as it is.
> B: However, _____
> A: Yeah, it could. Delaying it doesn't make it any easier.
> B: Good call! The sooner begun, the sooner done.

① it takes courage to see a dentist.
② how about taking it easy?
③ allow time to get over the illness.
④ what if it get worse than that?

123. 밑줄 친 부분에 들어갈 말로 가장 적절한 것은?

> To resolve the conflict between the two departments, the manager _____ a discussion to find a mutually acceptable solution.

① ignored   ② escalated
③ mediated   ④ postponed

121

해석 그녀는 결과에 불공정하게 영향을 주는 것을 피하기 위해 그 논란이 많은 제안에 대한 투표를 기권하기로 결정했다.

어휘 vote 투표하다   controversial 논란이 많은   proposal 제안
avoid 피하다   outcome 결과   unfairly 불공정하게
recover 회복하다   investigate 조사하다   rescue 구조하다
abstain 기권하다

근거

> She decided to relinquish voting on the controversial proposal to avoid influencing the outcome unfairly.

정답 ④

주요 어휘 정리

abstain 기권하다, 포기하다	investigate 조사하다	
= renounce	= inspect	look into
forsake	scrutinize	delve into
forgo	examine	probe into
give up		go over
		pore over

123

해석 두 부서 간의 갈등을 해결하기 위해, 매니저는 서로 수용할 수 있는 해결책을 찾기 위한 논의를 중재했다.

어휘 resolve 해결하다   conflict 갈등   department 부서
discussion 논의   mutually 서로   acceptable 수용할 수 있는
ignore 무시하다   escalate 확대시키다   mediate 중재하다
postpone 연기하다

근거

> To resolve the conflict between the two departments, the manager mediated a discussion to find a mutually acceptable solution.

정답 ③

주요 어휘 정리

escalate 확대시키다	mediate 중재하다
= grow	= arbitrate
develop	conciliate
increase	

122

> A: 어머! 나 이가 흔들려.
> B: 진짜? 너무 늦기 전에 치과에 가야 해.
> A: 아니야. 그냥 이대로 둘래.
> B: 하지만, 그보다 더 나빠지면 어떻게 해?
> A: 그래, 그럴 수도 있겠다. 그걸 미룬다고 그게 더 쉬워지는 건 아니니까.
> B: 좋은 결정이야! 매도 먼저 맞는 게 나아.

① 치과에 가는 건 용기가 필요해.
② 마음을 편히 먹는 게 어때?
③ 질병에서 회복할 시간을 줘.

어휘 delay 미루다   good call 좋은 결정
The sooner begun, the sooner done. 매도 먼저 맞는 게 낫다.
courage 용기   take it easy 마음을 편히 먹다
get over ~에서 회복하다   illness 질병

정답 ④

DAY 13

124 밑줄 친 부분에 들어갈 말로 가장 적절한 것은?

> A: Hey, I heard there's a new ramen place that just opened downtown.
> B: Yeah! I saw it on social media — looks amazing.
> A: Should we go this weekend? I think it's getting popular fast.
> B: _____.
> A: Wow, that long? Maybe we should get there early.
> B: They open at 11, so arriving early really helps.

① They're open from 1 PM to 9 PM every day
② Their specialty is miso ramen with roasted garlic
③ The wait time can be over an hour during weekends
④ They have another branch opening next month

125 밑줄 친 부분에 들어갈 말로 가장 적절한 것은?

> The success of fraudsters often does hinge on their ability to tell a convincing story. They make up pretty _____ stories to get what they want.

① persuasive   ② unrealistic
③ frequent   ④ distorted

126 밑줄 친 부분에 들어갈 말로 가장 적절한 것은?

> A: Did you watch the game last night? Wasn't it exciting?
> B: Yeah, it was very intense!
> A: _____
> B: That's when they scored those last-minute points. It was crazy!
> A: Right! It was such a nail-biter.

① When was the game broadcast on the television?
② I couldn't believe they didn't make the comeback.
③ I was not sure whether they could win or not.
④ Which part of that game was the most exciting?

124

> A: 야, 시내에 새로운 라멘집이 생겼대.
> B: 응! 나도 SNS에서 봤어 — 엄청 맛있어 보이더라.
> A: 이번 주말에 가볼까? 금방 인기 많아질 것 같아.
> B: 주말에는 대기 시간이 한 시간 넘게 걸릴 수도 있어.
> A: 와, 그렇게 오래 기다려야 해? 그럼 일찍 가야겠다.
> B: 11시에 문 여니까 일찍 가면 진짜 도움이 돼

① 매일 오후 1시부터 9시까지 영업해
② 대표 메뉴는 구운 마늘이 들어간 미소 라멘이야
④ 다음 달에 다른 지점도 연대

[어휘] downtown 시내에 specialty 대표 메뉴 roasted 구운
wait time 대기 시간 branch 지점

[정답] ③

125

[해석] 사기꾼의 성공은 설득력 있는 이야기를 하는 능력에 종종 달려있다. 그들은 자신들이 원하는 것을 얻기 위해 매우 설득력 있는 이야기를 지어낸다.

[어휘] fraudster 사기꾼 hinge on ~에 달려 있다
convincing 설득력 있는 make up 지어내다
persuasive 설득력 있는 unrealistic 비현실적인 frequent 잦은
distorted 왜곡된

[근거]

> The success of fraudsters often does hinge on their ability to tell a convincing story. They make up pretty persuasive stories to get what they want.

[정답] ①

[주요 어휘 정리]
persuasive 설득력 있는
= convincing
  compelling
  credible

126

> A: 어젯밤 그 경기 봤어? 재미있지 않았어?
> B: 응, 정말 강렬한 경기였어!
> A: 그 경기의 어느 부분이 제일 재미있었어?
> B: 바로 그들이 마지막 순간에 점수를 득점했을 때였어. 엄청났어!
> A: 맞아. 정말 손에 땀을 쥐게 했어.

① 그 경기가 언제 텔레비전으로 중계되었어?
② 그들이 열세를 만회하지 못했다니 믿을 수가 없었어.
③ 나는 그들이 이길지 질지 확신하지 못했어.

[어휘] intense 강렬한 score 득점하다 last-minute 마지막 순간의
nail-biter 손에 땀을 쥐게 하는 경기[영화, 이야기]
broadcast 중계하다 comeback 열세의 만회

[정답] ④

127 밑줄 친 부분에 들어갈 말로 가장 적절한 것은?

> On one hand, I admit I'm not good at managing money. But on the other, I never want to be as _____ as my partner who is an extreme saver.

① lively   ② frugal
③ prodigal   ④ conscientious

128 밑줄 친 부분에 들어갈 말로 가장 적절한 것은?

> Journalists must be _____. For instance, they must be good at writing, listening to people, speaking, working quickly, and doing research.

① rigid   ② contemporary
③ extensive   ④ versatile

127

해석 한편으로, 나는 내가 돈 관리에 서툴다는 것을 인정한다. 그러나 다른 한편으로는, 나는 절대 지나친 절약가인 내 배우자처럼 절약하고 싶지 않다.

어휘 extreme 지나친 lively 활기 넘치는 frugal 절약하는
prodigal 사치스러운 conscientious 양심적인

근거

> On one hand, I admit I'm not good at managing money. But on the other, I never want to be as frugal as my partner who is an extreme saver.

정답 ②

주요 어휘 정리

frugal 절약하는, 검소한
= thrifty
  economical

prodigal 사치스러운, 낭비하는
= wasteful
  lavish
  extravagant
  luxurious

128

해석 기자는 다재다능해야 한다. 예를 들어, 그들은 글을 쓰는 것, 사람들의 말을 듣는 것, 말하는 것, 신속히 일하는 것, 조사를 하는 것에 능숙해야 한다.

어휘 journalist 기자 be good at ~에 능숙하다 rigid 엄격한
contemporary 동시대의 extensive 아주 넓은
versatile 다재다능한

근거

> Journalists must be versatile. For instance, they must be good at writing, listening to people, speaking, working quickly, and doing research.

정답 ④

주요 어휘 정리

rigid 엄격한, 엄한
= strict
  rigorous
  stern
  stringent

versatile 다재다능한
= well-rounded
  all-around
  all-purpose

129 밑줄 친 부분에 들어갈 말로 가장 적절한 것은??

> A good barista, or a coffee professional, has to have a _____ sense of taste as well as smell to distinguish between different flavors and aromas.

① blunt
② spare
③ clumsy
④ keen

130 밑줄 친 부분에 들어갈 말로 가장 적절한 것은?

Emma Thomson
Hey, do you have any vacation plans coming up?
10:42

Jake Miller
Hi Emma! Yes, I'm planning a trip to Hawaii next month. How about you?
10:43

Emma Thomson
I'm thinking of going to Italy later this year. Any specific places you're excited to visit in Hawaii?
10:44

Jake Miller
Definitely! The beaches in Maui and Volcanoes National Park. _____?
10:45

Emma Thomson
Exploring Rome and visiting the Colosseum, and of course, enjoying the food.
10:46

Jake Miller
Have a fantastic trip!
10:47

Emma Thomson
Thanks! You too. Let's share stories when we're back.
10:48

① What are you looking forward to in Italy
② What's the best accommodation you've stayed in
③ Do you have any travel tips for staying safe abroad
④ How do you manage your budget while traveling

129

[해석] 훌륭한 바리스타, 즉 커피 전문가는 다양한 맛과 향을 분간하기 위해 예민한 후각 뿐 아니라 미각도 가지고 있어야만 한다.

[어휘] professional 전문가 distinguish 분간하다 flavor 맛 aroma 향 blunt 무딘 spare 여분의, 남는, 여가의; 아끼다 clumsy 서툰 keen 예민한

[근거]

> A good barista, or a coffee professional, has to have a <u>keen</u> sense of taste as well as smell to <u>distinguish between different flavors and aromas</u>.

[정답] ④

[주요 어휘 정리]

blunt 무딘 ↔ keen 예민한 / 날카로운
= dull   = sensitive = sharp
                            acute

clumsy 서툰
= poor
  inept
  maladroit
  all thumbs

130

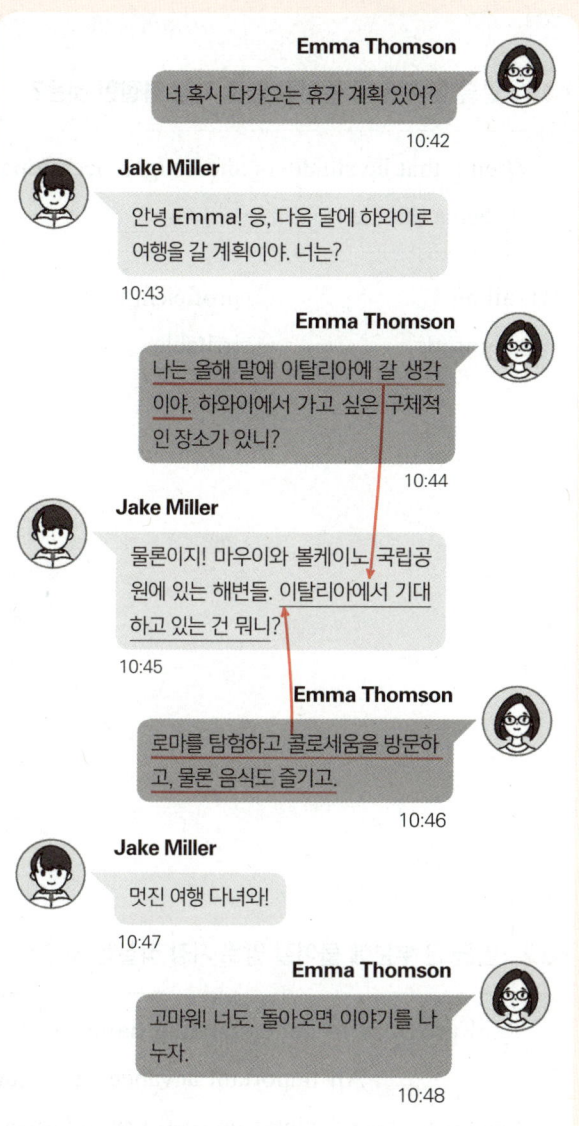

② 너가 묵었던 최고의 숙소는 어디야
③ 해외에서 안전하게 지낼 수 있는 여행 팁이 있니
④ 여행 중에 예산을 어떻게 관리하니

[어휘] vacation 휴가 come up 다가오다 specific 구체적인 definitely 분명히 explore 탐험하다 fantastic 멋진 accommodation 숙소 abroad 해외에서

[정답] ①

131 밑줄 친 부분에 들어갈 말로 가장 적절한 것은?

> Seeing that he shudders and coughs occasionally, it seems that he is _____.

① ailing   ② proficient
③ vigorous   ④ irritable

132 밑줄 친 부분에 들어갈 말로 가장 적절한 것은?

> Real progress in understanding nature is rarely _____. All important advances are sudden intuitions, new principles, and new ways of seeing.

① incremental   ② abrupt
③ ingenious   ④ temporary

133 밑줄 친 부분에 들어갈 말로 가장 적절한 것은?

Ella Blake
Hello! I'd like to order some macarons for this afternoon. Is that possible?
10:42

Dessert Shop
Hello! Yes, of course. What flavors would you like?
10:43

Ella Blake
I'd like 3 vanilla, 3 chocolate, 3 raspberry, and 3 pistachio, please.
10:44

Dessert Shop
Sure, that's 12 macarons in total. _____?
10:45

Ella Blake
Yes, could you please package them as a gift? And can I pick them up around 3 PM?
10:46

Dessert Shop
Got it. I'll prepare them with gift packaging. They'll be ready by 3 PM. Thank you!
10:47

Ella Blake
Thank you!
10:48

① Could you share any feedback
② Are there any other flavors you want to try
③ Are there any dietary restrictions or allergies
④ Do you have any specific requests on this order

131

[해석] 가끔 몸을 떨고 기침하는 걸 보니 그는 병든 것 같다.

[어휘] shudder 몸을 떨다 cough 기침하다 occasionally 가끔
ailing 병든 proficient 능숙한 vigorous 활기찬
irritable 짜증을 잘 내는

[근거]

Seeing that he shudders and coughs occasionally, it seems that he is ailing.

[정답] ①

[주요 어휘 정리]
ailing 병든
= ill
  unwell
  sick

132

[해석] 자연을 이해하는 것에 있어 진정한 진보는 거의 점진적이지 않다. 모든 중요한 발전은 갑작스러운 직관, 새로운 원리, 그리고 새로운 시각에서 왔다.

[어휘] progress 진보 advance 발전 sudden 갑작스러운
intuition 직관 principle 원리 incremental 점진적인
abrupt 갑작스러운 ingenious 독창적인 temporary 일시적인

[근거]

Real progress in understanding nature is rarely incremental. All important advances are sudden intuitions, new principles, and new ways of seeing.

[정답] ①

[주요 어휘 정리]

incremental 점진적인
= gradual
  progressive

ingenious 독창적인
= original
  innovative
  creative

abrupt 갑작스러운
= sudden

temporary
= momentary
  transitory
  fleeting
  provisional
  short-lived
  ephemeral

133

Ella Blake
안녕하세요! 오늘 오후에 마카롱을 주문하고 싶습니다. 가능한가요?
10:42

디저트 가게
안녕하세요! 네, 물론입니다. 어떤 맛으로 하시겠어요?
10:43

Ella Blake
바닐라 3개, 초콜릿 3개, 라즈베리 3개, 피스타치오 3개 주세요.
10:44

디저트 가게
네, 마카롱 총 12개입니다. 이 주문에 대한 구체적인 요청 사항이 있습니까?
10:45

Ella Blake
네, 선물용으로 포장해주실 수 있나요? 그리고 오후 3시쯤 찾으러 갈 수 있을까요?
10:46

디저트 가게
알겠습니다. 선물 포장으로 준비하겠습니다. 오후 3시까지 준비될 겁니다. 감사합니다!
10:47

Ella Blake
고마워요!
10:48

① 공유해주실 피드백이 있으신가요
② 맛보고 싶으신 다른 맛이 있나요
③ 식이 제한이나 알레르기가 있나요

[어휘] flavor 맛 package 포장하다 pick up 찾아가다
Got it. 알겠습니다. dietary 식이의 restriction 제한
allergy 알레르기 specific 구체적인 request 요청

[정답] ④

134 밑줄 친 부분에 들어갈 말로 가장 적절한 것은?

Erin Sullivan
Did you see the revised schedule for the project?
10:42

 Jason Kim
Yeah, and I can't believe the deadline is this Friday.
10:43

Erin Sullivan
I know. We barely have time to finish the report.
10:44

 Jason Kim

10:45

Erin Sullivan
True. I'll talk to the manager to see if we can get an extension.
10:46

 Jason Kim
Good idea. Otherwise, we're going to be rushing everything.
10:47

① Maybe we should ask for more time.
② The deadline was already extended last week.
③ I think I'll work remotely tomorrow.
④ Did you hear the manager praised our last report?

135 밑줄 친 부분에 들어갈 말로 가장 적절한 것은?

In order to _____ the financial crisis that is likely to unfold after retirement, people should be proactive and prepared for the life after retirement.

① overlook ② complicate
③ avoid   ④ exacerbate

134

② 마감일은 지난주에 이미 연장됐어.
③ 나 내일 재택근무 할 생각이야.
④ 매니저가 우리의 지난번 보고서를 칭찬했다는 얘기 들었어?

어휘 revise 수정하다 barely 거의 ~ 없이 extension 연장
extend 연장하다 work remotely 재택근무하다 praise 칭찬하다

정답 ①

135

해석 은퇴 후 일어날 가능성이 있는 재정 위기를 피하기 위해서, 사람들은 사전 대책을 강구하고 은퇴 후의 삶에 대해 준비해야 한다.

어휘 financial 재정의 crisis 위기 unfold 일어나다
retirement 은퇴 proactive 사전 대책을 강구하는
overlook 간과하다 complicate 복잡하게 만들다 avoid 피하다
exacerbate 악화시키다

근거

> In order to avoid the financial crisis that is likely to unfold after retirement, people should be proactive and prepared for the life after retirement.

정답 ③

주요 어휘 정리

overlook 간과하다, 무시하다	avoid 피하다
= ignore	= shun
neglect	avert
disregard	eschew
	evade
	circumvent

exacerbate 악화시키다 ↔ alleviate 완화하다
= aggravate   = reduce
  make worse   relieve
  worsen   relax
                    soothe

DAY 14 117

136 밑줄 친 부분에 들어갈 말로 가장 적절한 것은?

> A: Have you noticed any changes in the company's policies lately?
> B: Yes, I have. They've updated the remote work policy to allow more flexibility.
> A: That's true. I've also heard they're planning to introduce a new performance review system next quarter.
> B: Really? In what way do you think the review system will change?
> A: It's not certain, but from what I heard, _____.
> B: That sounds promising. I'm looking forward to seeing how it works out.

① because of it, our salaries will freeze
② it will be more comprehensive and fair
③ we need to demonstrate better performance
④ welfare payments will be gradually reduced

137 밑줄 친 부분에 들어갈 말로 가장 적절한 것은?

Daniel
Hey, did you check the shared folder today?
10:42

 Emily
No, what should I be looking at?
10:43

Daniel
I uploaded the draft of the monthly sales report. I'm a bit worried I might have missed something.
10:44

 Emily
You know _____. Right?
10:45

Daniel
Yeah, I checked with the team and updated the numbers.
10:46

 Emily
Nice job. I'll take a closer look later.
10:47

① you need to include the latest figures from the marketing team
② you need to send the report on the missing items to the client
③ when you should update the numbers for the attendance sheet
④ how you add a summary at the beginning of the report

136

A: 최근 회사 정책에 어떤 변화가 있는 것을 눈치채셨나요?
B: 네, 눈치챘어요. 유연성을 높이기 위해 원격 근무 정책을 업데이트했잖아요.
A: 맞아요. 다음 분기에 새로운 성과 평가 시스템을 도입할 계획이라는 것도 들었어요.
B: 정말요? 그 평가 시스템이 어떤 식으로 달라질 것이라 생각하세요?
A: 확실하지는 않지만, 제가 들은 바로는, 더 포괄적이고 공정해질 거예요.
B: 그거 희망적으로 들리네요. 어떻게 잘 될지 보는 것이 기대돼요.

① 그것 때문에, 우리 봉급이 동결될 거예요
③ 우리는 더 나은 성과를 보여줘야 할 필요가 있어요
④ 복지 수당이 점차 줄어들 거예요

어휘 policy 정책 remote work 원격 근무 flexibility 유연성 introduce 도입하다 performance 성과 quarter 분기 promising 희망적인 work out 잘 되다 salary 봉급 freeze 동결되다 comprehensive 포괄적인 demonstrate 보여주다 welfare payments 복지 수당 gradually 점차 reduce 줄이다

정답 ②

137

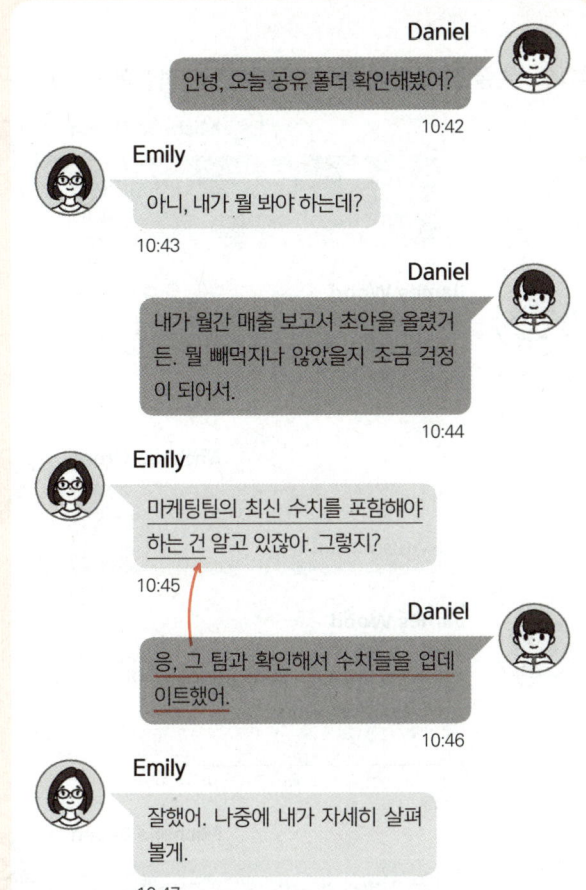

② 고객에게 누락 항목에 관한 보고서를 보내야 하는 건
③ 언제 출근부 수치를 업데이트해야 하는지
④ 보고서 시작 부분에 요약본을 어떻게 추가하는지

어휘 shared 공유된 upload 올리다 draft 초안 take a look 한 번 보다 figure 수치 client 고객 attendance sheet 출근부 summary 요약본

정답 ①

138 밑줄 친 부분에 들어갈 말로 가장 적절한 것은?

Michelle Green
James, have you seen the email about the office party next week?
10:42

 James Wood
Yes, I did. Are you planning to attend?
10:43

Michelle Green
Definitely. Are we supposed to bring anything?
10:44

James Wood
It says we can bring snacks or drinks if we want. _____
10:45

Michelle Green
Sounds good. I'll bring snacks, and you can bring drinks?
10:46

 James Wood
Perfect. I'll pick up some drinks on my way in.
10:47

① Let's divide the roles.
② I'll take care of everything.
③ How much did you pay for snacks?
④ What do you prefer to drink?

139 밑줄 친 부분에 들어갈 말로 가장 적절한 것은?

A: My throat is really dry.
B: Do you want to go get something to drink?
A: Let's do that.
B: What did you want to drink?
A: I was thinking about getting some soda.
B: _____.
A: What else should I drink then?
B: Water is what's best for you.
A: I guess I will get water.

① Just wait here and I'll just get you a soda
② Oh, no! This vending machine is out of order now
③ You shouldn't drink a soda when you're really thirsty
④ A soda is so refreshing on a hot day

140 밑줄 친 부분에 들어갈 말로 가장 적절한 것은?

The hardship of beggars on city streets and the _____ of the homeless may inspire sympathy, for the same reason.

① charity   ② fortune
③ plight   ④ dearth

138

② 내가 다 책임질게.
③ 간식에 얼마를 지불했어?
④ 어떤 음료를 선호해?

어휘 attend 참석하다 pick up 사 가다 take care of ~을 책임지다

정답 ①

139

A: 나 목이 너무 말라.
B: 뭐 좀 마시러 갈래?
A: 그러자.
B: 뭐 마시고 싶었어?
A: 나는 탄산음료를 마실까 생각 중이었어.
B: 너는 진짜 목마를 때 탄산음료는 마시지 말아야 해.
A: 그럼 다른 어떤 걸 마셔야 해?
B: 물이 너한테 가장 좋아.
A: 물을 마셔야겠다.

① 여기서 기다리면 내가 탄산음료를 가져다줄게
② 아, 안 돼! 이 자판기 지금 고장 났어
④ 탄산음료는 더운 날 정말 상쾌하지

어휘 soda 탄산음료 vending machine 자판기 out of order 고장 난 refreshing 상쾌한

정답 ③

140

해석 도시 거리의 거지들의 어려움과 노숙자의 곤경은 같은 이유로 동정심을 불러일으키는 것 같다.

어휘 hardship 어려움 beggar 거지 the homeless 노숙자 inspire 불러일으키다 charity 자선 fortune 행운 plight 곤경 dearth 부족

근거

The hardship of beggars on city streets and the plight of the homeless may inspire sympathy, for the same reason.

정답 ③

주요 어휘 정리

plight 곤경, 역경	dearth 부족, 결핍
= trouble	= lack
difficulty	insufficiency
dilemma	shortage
difficult situation	deficiency
predicament	scarcity
quandary	

141 밑줄 친 부분에 들어갈 말로 가장 적절한 것은?

Emily Johnson
Do you remember Kevin's school concert is tomorrow?
10:44

Mark Johnson
Oh, right! It's tomorrow!
10:45

Emily Johnson
Didn't you say you have an important meeting tomorrow?
10:46

Mark Johnson
Yes, I did. It was impossible to reschedule it.
10:47

Emily Johnson
That's okay. I'll record his performance so you won't miss a thing.
10:48

Mark Johnson
Thanks. If the meeting ends early, I might be able to be there by four.
10:49

Emily Johnson
_____
10:50

Mark Johnson
At least, I can pick you guys up and go home together.
10:51

① Great. We need a ride to the concert hall.
② Right. I'll buy a new camera this afternoon.
③ What for? The concert will be over by then.
④ No way! Postpone the meeting for our son.

142 밑줄 친 부분에 들어갈 말로 가장 적절한 것은?

Most Americans were _____ with the Cubans, viewing their struggle for independence with empathy, but President Cleveland was determined to preserve neutrality.

① unfeeling
② indifferent
③ unfriendly
④ sympathetic

141

Emily Johnson
내일 Kevin의 학교 콘서트인 것 기억해?
10:44

Mark Johnson
아, 맞아! 내일이네!
10:45

Emily Johnson
내일 중요한 회의가 있다고 하지 않았어?
10:46

Mark Johnson
응, 그랬지. 일정을 변경하는 건 불가능했어.
10:47

Emily Johnson
괜찮아. 내가 그의 공연을 녹화해서 당신이 하나도 놓치지 않도록 할게.
10:48

Mark Johnson
고마워. 회의가 일찍 끝나면 4시까지 그곳에 갈 수 있을 지도 몰라.
10:49

Emily Johnson
뭐하러? 콘서트는 그때쯤 끝날 텐데.
10:50

Mark Johnson
적어도, 당신이랑 Kevin을 차에 태우고 집에 같이 갈 수는 있잖아.
10:51

① 좋아. 우린 콘서트장으로 갈 차편이 필요해.
② 맞아. 나는 오늘 오후에 새 카메라를 살 거야.
④ 안 돼! 우리 아들을 위해서 회의를 연기해.

[어휘] reschedule 일정을 변경하다   record 녹화하다
performance 공연   pick up ~을 태우다   ride 차편
postpone 미루다

[정답] ③

142

[해석] 대부분의 미국인은 쿠바인에게 동정적이었고, 그들의 독립을 위한 투쟁을 공감하며 보았지만, 클리블랜드 대통령은 중립을 지키기로 결심했다.

[어휘] Cuban 쿠바인   struggle 투쟁   independence 독립
empathy 공감   president 대통령
be determined to ~하기로 결심하다   preserve 지키다
neutrality 중립   unfeeling 냉정한   indifferent 무관심한
unfriendly 불친절한   sympathetic 동정적인

[근거]

> Most Americans were sympathetic with the Cubans, viewing their struggle for independence with empathy, but President Cleveland was determined to preserve neutrality.

[정답] ④

[주요 어휘 정리]
sympathetic 동정적인
= pitiful
  compassionate

143 밑줄 친 부분에 들어갈 말로 가장 적절한 것은?

> A: We're running late for the movie.
> B: I know, traffic's terrible.
> A: Step on it. We're going to miss the beginning.
> B: I'm trying, but these cars aren't moving.
> A: Do you have any good idea?
> B: _____.
> A: I heard its construction has been completed. That'll get us there faster.

① The side streets should have been mended quickly
② I think we should give up going to the theater
③ I would rather be late than not get there at all
④ Let's take a detour and pass the newly-built tunnel

144 밑줄 친 부분에 들어갈 말로 가장 적절한 것은?

Sophie
Have you tried that new Italian restaurant in town?
10:42

 Matt
Not yet, but I've heard that it's good. Have you?
10:43

Sophie
Yeah, I went there yesterday. The pasta was amazing!
10:44

 Matt
_____.
10:45

Sophie
I'm down! How about Friday night?
10:46

 Matt
Friday works. Let's say 7 PM?
10:47

Sophie
Perfect. I'll make a reservation.
10:48

 Matt
Great! Looking forward to it.
10:49

① The Italian pasta is my comfort food
② Reservation is needed in that case
③ We should go together sometime, then
④ The store is always full on Fridays

143

> A: 영화에 늦겠어.
> B: 맞아, 교통체증이 심해.
> A: 속도를 내봐, 시작 부분을 놓치겠어.
> B: 노력하고 있는데, 이 차들이 움직이질 않아.
> A: 좋은 생각 있어?
> B: 우회해서 새로 세운 터널을 통과하자.
> A: 그것의 건설이 완성되었다는 건 들었어. 그러면 더 빨리 도착하겠다.

① 옆길은 빠르게 수리되었어야 해.
② 극장 가는 건 포기하는 게 좋을 것 같아
③ 거기 아예 못 가니 늦게 가는 게 낫지

어휘 run late 늦다   traffic 교통   Step on it. 속도를 내봐.
construction 건설   complete 완성하다   mend 수리하다
take a detour 우회하다

정답 ④

144

① 이탈리아식 파스타는 나를 편하게 하는 음식이에요
② 그런 경우라면 예약이 필요해요
④ 그 가게는 금요일이면 항상 가득 차요

어휘 I'm down! 나도 좋아!   comfort food 편하게 하는 음식

정답 ③

DAY 15 125

145 밑줄 친 부분에 들어갈 말로 가장 적절한 것은?

> A: I'm supposed to meet with you at 1:30.
> B: Yes, I see. What did you need to see me about?
> A: There's a problem with my schedule. _____.
> B: Oh, I see.
> A: Is it at all possible for you to fix that error?
> B: No problem. Let me see if I can find one of these classes on another day.
> A: I would greatly appreciate that.

① Two of my classes occur at the same time
② I signed up too many credits for this semester
③ My math professor is strict in grading
④ I have to take a year off from school

146 밑줄 친 부분에 들어갈 말로 가장 적절한 것은?

> Most legal strategies assume that the _____ evidence is final; however, this doesn't account for new conclusive findings that may emerge during the trial.

① incessant   ② subsequent
③ versatile   ④ preliminary

147 밑줄 친 부분에 들어갈 말로 가장 적절한 것은?

> Both the frogs and toads survived the mass extinction event that _____ the dinosaurs they shared the land with.

① supported   ② contributed
③ exterminated ④ fortified

145

> A: 1시 반에 당신과 면담하기로 되어 있는데요.
> B: 네, 그렇군요. 무슨 일 때문에 저를 보자 하셨죠?
> A: 제 시간표에 문제가 있어서요. 제 수업 중에 두 수업이 같은 시간에 있습니다.
> B: 아, 그렇군요.
> A: 혹시 그 오류를 고치는 게 가능할까요?
> B: 문제없어요. 이 수업 중 하나가 다른 날에도 있는지 볼게요.
> A: 그렇게 해주시면 대단히 감사하겠습니다.

② 이번 학기에 너무 많은 학점을 신청했어요
③ 제 수학 교수님이 평가에 엄격해요
④ 1년 휴학을 해야 해요

어휘 schedule 시간표   sign up 신청하다   credit 학점   strict 엄격한
grading 평가   take a year off from school 1년 휴학하다

정답 ①

146

해석 대부분의 법률 전략은 예비 증거가 최종적인 것으로 가정한다; 그러나, 이는 재판 과정에서 드러날 수 있는 새로운 결정적인 발견을 고려하지 못한다.

어휘 strategy 전략   assume 가정하다   evidence 증거
account for ~을 고려하다   conclusive 결정적인   finding 발견
emerge 드러나다   trial 재판   incessant 끊임없는
subsequent 차후의   versatile 다재다능한   preliminary 예비의

근거

> Most legal strategies assume that the preliminary evidence is final; however, this doesn't account for new conclusive findings that may emerge during the trial.

정답 ④

주요 어휘 정리
versatile 다재다능한	preliminary 예비의
= all-round	= introductory
multi-talented	preparatory
well-rounded	

147

해석 개구리와 두꺼비 둘 다 그들이 땅을 공유했던 공룡들을 없애 버린 대멸종 사건에서 살아남았다.

어휘 toad 두꺼비   survive ~에서 살아남다   extinction 멸종
support 지지하다   contribute 기여하다
exterminate 근절하다   fortify 강화하다

근거

> Both the frogs and toads survived the mass extinction event that exterminated the dinosaurs they shared the land with.

정답 ③

주요 어휘 정리
exterminate 근절하다		fortify 강화하다
= destroy	root out	= strengthen
eradicate	sweep out	reinforce
eliminate		intensify
remove		consolidate
get rid of		beef up
wipe out		

148 밑줄 친 부분에 들어갈 말로 가장 적절한 것은?

> After hours of slow cooking, the meat became so _____ that it could be easily cut with a fork.

① spoiled ② humid
③ tender   ④ tough

149 빈칸에 들어갈 말로 가장 적절한 것은?

> With pouring rain that didn't seem to _____ anytime soon, the couple went around knocking doors, asking for shelter.

① diminish ② increase
③ amplify   ④ worsen

150 밑줄 친 부분에 들어갈 말로 가장 적절한 것은?

Mila Brooks: Hi, Dr. Johnson. You know my son, Ben? (10:42)

Dr. Johnson: Sure. I saw him at family counseling before. (10:43)

Mila Brooks: I'm worried about him these days. He wakes up in the middle of the night and won't stop crying. (10:44)

Dr. Johnson: I'm sure you've been busy taking care of the baby, and it probably makes Ben feel stressed. (10:45)

Mila Brooks: Oh, I don't play with Ben as much as I used to. That could explain his behavior. (10:46)

Dr. Johnson: Now, you know what Ben needs. (10:47)

Mila Brooks: _____ (10:48)

① Right. You can ignore his selfish and rude behavior
② I see. You need to encourage him to fall asleep on his own
③ Yes. I should make time each day to spend with him
④ Certainly. I'll ask him to share his toys with his brother

148

해석 여러 시간 동안 천천히 조리한 후, 고기는 매우 부드러워져서 포크로도 쉽게 잘릴 수 있게 되었다.

어휘 meat 고기 spoiled 상한 humid 습한 tender 부드러운 tough 질긴

근거
After hours of slow cooking, the meat became so tender that it could be easily cut with a fork.

정답 ③

149

해석 금세 약해질 것 같지 않은 장대비로 인해, 그 부부는 주변의 문을 두드리며 잠시 비 피할 곳을 요청했다.

어휘 shelter 잠시 비를 피하는 곳 diminish 약해지다 increase 증가하다 amplify 확대되다 worsen 악화되다

근거
With pouring rain that didn't seem to diminish anytime soon, the couple went around knocking doors, asking for shelter.

정답 ①

주요 어휘 정리
diminish 약해지다, 줄어들다
= weaken
  decrease
  dwindle
  decline
  wane

150

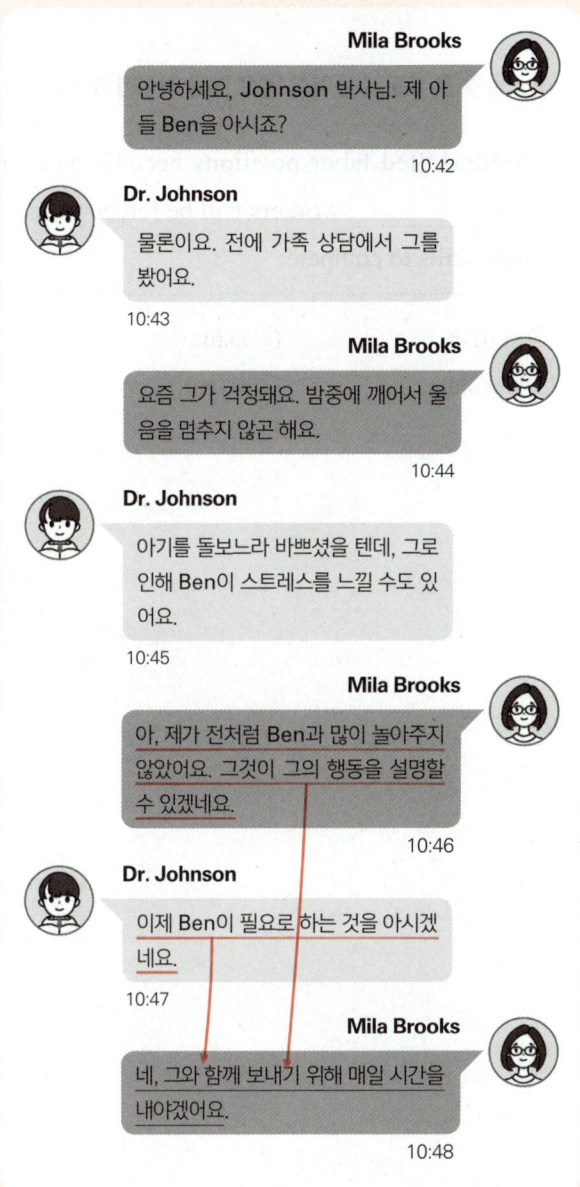

① 맞아요. 그의 이기적이고 무례한 행동은 무시하셔도 돼요
② 그렇군요. 당신은 그가 혼자서 잠들도록 격려해야 해요
④ 물론이죠. 저는 그가 그의 장난감을 남동생과 공유하도록 부탁할게요

어휘 counseling 상담 be busy -ing ~하느라 바쁘다
take care of ~을 돌보다 stressed 스트레스 받는
explain 설명하다 behavior 행동 ignore 무시하다
selfish 이기적인 rude 무례한 encourage 격려하다
fall asleep 잠들다 on one's own 혼자서
make time 시간을 내다 share 공유하다

정답 ③

151 밑줄 친 부분에 들어갈 말로 가장 적절한 것은?

> As unskilled labor positions become more and more _____, workers will be forced to acquire new skills to compete.

① selfish ② astute
③ obsolete ④ novel

152 밑줄 친 부분에 들어갈 말로 가장 적절한 것은?

 Austin Blake
Hey! The weather lately has been amazing. I really want to go camping!
10:42

 Carrie Bradshaw
Hi! Yeah, I've been itching to go camping too.
10:43

 Austin Blake
If we go to the mountains, we can do some trekking, or go to a river for fishing!
10:44

 Carrie Bradshaw
That sounds perfect! And we can also make a campfire at night.
10:45

 Austin Blake
_____?
10:46

 Carrie Bradshaw
A weekend would be ideal for everyone to go camping. How about next weekend?
10:47

 Austin Blake
Sounds good! Let's go next weekend then. I'm really looking forward to it!
10:48

① When would be a good time
② When have you been camping before
③ What's your favorite activity to do while camping
④ When would you like to make camping plan

151

[해석] 기술이 필요하지 않은 노동직이 점점 더 구식이 됨에 따라, 노동자들은 경쟁하기 위해 새로운 기술을 습득해야 할 것이다.

[어휘] unskilled 기술이 필요하지 않은 acquire 습득하다
compete 경쟁하다 selfish 이기적인 astute 기민한
obsolete 구식의 novel 새로운

[근거]

> As unskilled labor positions become more and more obsolete, workers will be forced to acquire new skills to compete.

[정답] ③

[주요 어휘 정리]

astute 기민한
= agile   shrewd
  canny   speedy
  nimble   rapid

obsolete 구식의 ↔ up-to-date 최신의
= outdated   = latest
  old-fashioned   newest
  out of date

152

 Austin Blake
야! 요즘 날씨가 너무 좋아. 나는 정말 캠핑을 가고 싶어!
10:42

 Carrie Bradshaw
안녕! 응, 나도 캠핑 가고 싶어 근질거렸어.
10:43

 Austin Blake
우리가 산에 간다면 트레킹을 할 수 있고, 또는 낚시를 하러 강가에서 갈 수 있어!
10:44

 Carrie Bradshaw
딱 좋은데! 그리고 밤에 캠프파이어도 할 수 있어.
10:45

 Austin Blake
언제가 좋을까?
10:46

 Carrie Bradshaw
주말은 모두가 캠핑 가기에 이상적일 거야. 다음 주말은 어때?
10:47

 Austin Blake
좋아! 그럼 다음 주말에 가자. 정말 기대돼!
10:48

② 전에 언제 캠핑을 가봤어
③ 캠핑할 때 가장 좋아하는 활동이 뭐야
④ 언제 캠핑 계획을 세우고 싶어

[어휘] lately 요즘 amazing 너무 좋은
itch (몹시 ~하고 싶어) 근질거리다
trekking 트레킹: 산이나 계곡 따위를 다니는 도보 여행
ideal 이상적인

[정답] ①

153 밑줄 친 부분에 들어갈 말로 가장 적절한 것은?

> Blue-green algae can produce a toxin that can be _____ to pets.

① enigmatic ② deadly
③ secular ④ beneficial

154 밑줄 친 부분에 들어갈 말로 가장 적절한 것은?

> When it comes to moonlighting, it is not always about earning a few more extra bucks. People _____ a second job as a backup when they are insecure about their present job.

① adapt ② extract
③ commence ④ remove

155 밑줄 친 부분에 들어갈 말로 가장 적절한 것은?

> A: I'm in 507. I have a problem with my room.
> B: What is the problem, sir?
> A: There are cockroaches in my room.
> B: Are you sure, sir? Flies, I could believe, but cockroaches?
> A: I've counted nine different cockroaches, and I accidentally stepped on another one.
> B: Sir, _____.
> A: You dare to doubt me?
> B: I'm sorry, sir. Let me transfer you to my supervisor.

① we tried in vain to address the cockroach problem
② you are not eligible to flatter yourself in this case
③ I'm sorry that your room is not made up and ready
④ this hotel passed a thorough insect inspection perfectly

문장 분석 및 해설

153

[해석] 남조류는 반려동물에게 치명적일 수 있는 독소를 만들어낼 수 있다.

[어휘] blue-green algae 남조류 toxin 독소 enigmatic 불가사의한
deadly 치명적인 secular 세속적인 beneficial 이로운

[근거]

> Blue-green algae can produce a toxin that can be deadly to pets.

[정답] ②

[주요 어휘 정리]

enigmatic 수수께끼 같은, 불가사의한	secular 세속적인, 일상의
= mysterious	= worldly
uncanny	everyday
inscrutable	earthly
cryptic	daily
	mundane
	routine

154

[해석] 부업에 관한 한, 항상 몇 달러를 더 버는 것과 관련된 것은 아니다. 사람들은 현재 일에 대해 불안할 때 예비용으로서 두 번째 직업을 시작한다.

[어휘] moonlighting (야간의) 부업 backup 예비(용) insecure 불안한
adapt 적응하다 extract 추출하다 commence 시작하다
remove 제거하다

[근거]

> When it comes to moonlighting, it is not always about earning a few more extra bucks. People commence a second job as a backup when they are insecure about their present job.

[정답] ③

[주요 어휘 정리]

adapt 적응하다	commence 시작하다
= adjust	= undertake
accommodate	initiate
	launch
	begin
	start

155

> A: 507호입니다. 제 방에 문제가 있어요.
> B: 무슨 문제죠, 고객님?
> A: 제 방에 바퀴벌레가 있어요.
> B: 확실하세요? 파리라면 믿겠지만, 바퀴벌레요?
> A: 제가 아홉 마리의 바퀴벌레를 셌고, 뜻하지 않게 다른 바퀴벌레를 밟았어요.
> B: 고객님, 이 호텔은 철저한 벌레 검사를 완벽하게 통과했습니다.
> A: 저를 의심하는 건가요?
> B: 죄송합니다, 고객님. 제 상사에게 연결해드리겠습니다.

① 저희는 바퀴벌레 문제를 해결하려고 노력했지만 허사였습니다
② 당신은 이 상황에서는 자만할 자격이 없습니다
③ 당신의 방이 정리되지 않고 준비되지 않은 것에 대해 죄송합니다

[어휘] cockroach 바퀴벌레 fly 파리 accidentally 뜻하지 않게
dare 감히 ~하다 doubt 의심하다 supervisor 상사
in vain 허사가 되어 address 해결하다 eligible 자격이 있는
flatter oneself 자만하다 make up a room 방을 정리하다
thorough 철저한 inspection 검사

[정답] ④

156 밑줄 친 부분에 들어갈 말로 가장 적절한 것은?

> With determination and perseverance, he was able to _____ his fear of public speaking.

① defend   ② shield
③ violate   ④ conquer

157 밑줄 친 부분에 들어갈 말로 가장 적절한 것은?

> Since dressing rooms were side by side, they decided to _____ the wall so they'd have one large room to themselves.

① build   ② demolish
③ seize   ④ suppress

158 밑줄 친 부분에 들어갈 말로 가장 적절한 것은?

> A: I've been feeling frustrated lately because of the lack of communication in our team.
> B: I get that. Communication is crucial for our success.
> A: Exactly. We really need clearer guidelines on project updates.
> B: What do you have in mind?
> A: We could have a weekly status meeting.
> B: _____
> A: I think team members take turns giving a presentation to inform others of the status of the project.
> B: Aha, it also helps the team stay on track for a project timeline, then.

① Our team also had a Monday meeting.
② I found myself in a complicated status.
③ How do you expect the meeting to go?
④ Who came up with the new guidelines?

156

해석 그는 결단력과 끈기로 대중 연설에 대한 두려움을 극복할 수 있었다.

어휘 determination 결단력 perseverance 끈기 fear 두려움
public speaking 대중 연설 defend 방어하다 shield 보호하다
violate 위반하다 conquer 극복하다

근거

> With determination and perseverance, he was able to conquer his fear of public speaking.

정답 ④

주요 어휘 정리

violate 위반하다	conquer 극복하다
= break	= overcome
breach	defeat
infringe	surmount
	get over

157

해석 탈의실이 나란히 있었기 때문에, 그들은 하나의 큰 방을 독차지하도록 벽을 허물기로 결정했다.

어휘 dressing room 탈의실 side by side 나란히 있는
have ~ to oneself ~을 독차지하다 build 세우다
demolish 허물다 seize 압수하다 suppress 진압하다

근거

> Since dressing rooms were side by side, they decided to demolish the wall so they'd have one large room to themselves.

정답 ②

주요 어휘 정리

demolish 허물다	suppress 진압하다
= pull down	= repress
tear down	control
	quell
	put down
	keep down

158

A: 요즘 우리 팀의 소통 부재로 답답해요.
B: 이해해요. 우리의 성공을 위해서는 의사소통이 중요해요.
A: 맞아요. 프로젝트 업데이트에 대한 더 명확한 지침이 필요해요.
B: 어떤 점을 염두에 두고 계신가요?
A: 주간 상황 회의를 할 수 있을 것 같아요.
B: 회의가 어떻게 진행될 거로 예상하세요?
A: 팀원들이 교대로 프레젠테이션을 해서 프로젝트의 상황을 다른 사람들에게 알리면 될 것 같아요.
B: 아하, 그러면, 팀이 프로젝트 일정을 계획대로 해나가는 데에도 도움이 되겠네요.

① 우리 팀도 월요일 회의를 했어요.
② 저는 복잡한 상황에 빠졌어요.
④ 누가 새로운 지침을 생각해 냈어요?

어휘 frustrated 답답한 lack 부재 status 상황 crucial 중요한
take turns 교대로 하다 inform 알리다
stay on track 계획대로 하다 complicated 복잡한
come up with ~을 생각해 내다

정답 ③

159 밑줄 친 부분에 들어갈 말로 가장 적절한 것은?

> A: Where would you like me to take you?
> B: I need to go to Gangnam Station.
> A: That's no problem. Please fasten your seat belt.
> B: How long is the ride?
> A: It'll be about 25 minutes.
> B: _____?
> A: That's as quick as I can do it.

① Can you get me there faster
② Is there any station near here
③ Is there any other way to get there
④ Can you take over the wheel

160 밑줄 친 부분에 들어갈 말로 가장 적절한 것은?

Anna Denver
Hey Mark, have you seen any good movies lately?
10:42

Mark Strong
Hi Anna! Yes, I watched *Dune* recently. It was visually stunning! How about you?
10:43

Anna Denver
I haven't seen *Dune* yet, but I heard it's amazing. I watched *No Time to Die* last week. Have you seen it?
10:44

Mark Strong
Yes, *No Time to Die* was fantastic! Daniel Craig really nailed it in his final Bond film. What did you think?
10:45

Anna Denver
_____.
10:46

Mark Strong
I agree with you. Well, let's catch up soon and maybe watch a movie together!
10:47

Anna Denver
Sounds like a plan!
10:48

① I struggled to stay awake through the entire film
② I definitely want to see it too because I heard it is really awesome
③ It was so boring that I found myself dozing off during the screening
④ The action scenes were thrilling, and the storyline kept me hooked throughout

159

A: 어디로 모셔다드릴까요?
B: 강남역으로 가주세요.
A: 문제 없습니다. 안전띠를 매주세요.
B: 얼마나 걸리나요?
A: 약 25분 걸립니다.
B: 더 빨리 갈 수 있을까요?
A: 이게 제가 할 수 있는 한 최대한 빨리 가는 겁니다.

② 여기 근처에 역이 있나요
③ 거기까지 가는 다른 길이 있나요
④ 대신 운전해줄 수 있나요

어휘 fasten one's seat belt 안전 벨트를 매다
take over the wheel 대신 운전하다

정답 ①

160

Anna Denver
이봐 Mark, 최근에 좋은 영화 본 적 있어?
10:42

Mark Strong
안녕 Anna! 응, 나는 최근에 <Dune>을 봤어. 그것은 시각적으로 굉장히 멋졌어! 너는 어때?
10:43

Anna Denver
나는 아직 <Dune>을 못 봤지만, 놀랍다고 들었어. 나는 지난주에 <No Time to Die>를 봤어. 너도 봤니?
10:44

Mark Strong
그래, <No Time to Die>는 환상적이었어! 다니엘 크레이그는 그의 마지막 본드 영화에서 정말로 잘했어. 어떻게 생각했어?
10:45

Anna Denver
액션 장면들은 짜릿했고, 줄거리는 내내 나를 빠져들게 했어.
10:46

Mark Strong
나도 네 말에 동의해. 그럼, 조만간 만나서 얘기도 하고 같이 영화 보자!
10:47

Anna Denver
좋은 생각이야!
10:48

① 나는 영화 내내 깨어 있으려고 애썼어
② 정말 멋지다고 해서 나도 꼭 보고 싶어
③ 너무 지루해서 상영 중에 졸았어

어휘 lately 최근에 recently 최근에 visually 시각적으로
stunning 굉장히 멋진 nail it 정말 잘하다
catch up soon 조만간 만나서 얘기하다 struggle 애쓰다
definitely 꼭 awesome 멋진 doze off 졸다
screening (영화) 상영 thrilling 짜릿한 storyline 줄거리
keep someone hooked ~를 빠져들게 하다 throughout 내내

정답 ④

DAY 17

161 밑줄 친 부분에 들어갈 말로 가장 적절한 것은?

> A: Have you read any good books lately?
> B: Yeah, I just finished a gripping mystery novel. It kept me on edge until the end.
> A: Those are the best kind. _____?
> B: I didn't see the identity of the culprit coming at all. It was cleverly written.
> A: Sounds like a page-turner. I'll add it to my reading list.

① How many points would you give the book
② What did you think of the book's pacing
③ What was the plot twist that surprised you
④ How did the setting influence the story

162 밑줄 친 부분에 들어갈 말로 가장 적절한 것은?

> _____ people can not only get through hard times but thrive during and after them. Just as a rubber ball rebounds after being squeezed, so do these people.

① Impatient   ② Reluctant
③ Susceptible ④ Resilient

163 밑줄 친 부분에 들어갈 말로 가장 적절한 것은?

> She was chosen to _____ her country in the upcoming international conference, where she showcased her expertise in diplomacy and economics.

① mislead   ② exploit
③ represent ④ encompass

161

A: 최근에 좋은 책 읽어본 것 있어?
B: 응, 방금 눈을 떼지 못하게 하는 추리소설을 다 읽었어. 그 책은 마지막까지 내가 계속 마음 졸이게 만들었어.
A: 그런 것들이 최고의 종류지. 너를 놀라게 한 줄거리의 뜻밖의 반전은 무엇이었어?
B: 난 범인의 정체를 전혀 예상하지 못했어. 그건 교묘하게 쓰여졌어.
A: 흥미진진한 책인 것 같네. 내 독서 목록에 그걸 추가해야겠어.

① 그 책에 몇 점을 주고 싶어
② 책의 전개 속도는 어땠다고 생각해
④ 배경이 어떻게 그 책에 영향을 주었어

어휘 gripping 눈을 떼지 못하게 하는   mystery novel 추리소설
on edge 마음 졸이는   identity 정체   culprit 범인
see ~ comig ~을 예상하다   cleverly 교묘하게
page-turner 흥미진진한 책   plot (이야기의)줄거리
twist 뜻밖의 반전   setting 배경

정답 ③

162

해석 회복력 있는 사람들은 힘든 시간을 극복할 수 있을 뿐만 아니라 그 시간 동안 그리고 그 후에도 잘 살 수 있다. 압박을 받은 후 고무공이 다시 튀어 오르듯, 이 사람들도 그렇다.

어휘 get through 극복하다   thrive 잘 살다   rubber ball 고무공
rebound 다시 튀어 오르다   squeeze 압박하다
impatient 참을성이 없는   reluctant 꺼리는   susceptible 취약한
resilient 회복력 있는

근거

Resilient people can not only get through hard times but thrive during and after them. Just as a rubber ball rebounds after being squeezed, so do these people.

정답 ④

주요 어휘 정리
susceptible 취약한   resilient 회복력 있는
= vulnerable   = flexible   plastic
                           elastic   supple
                           pliant   adaptable
                           pliable   adjustable

163

해석 그녀는 다가오는 국제회의에서 그녀의 나라를 대표하도록 선택되었고 그 곳에서 그녀는 외교와 경제 분야에서 그녀의 전문성을 보여주었다.

어휘 upcoming 다가오는   international 국제의   conference 회의
showcase 보여주다   expertise 전문성   diplomacy 외교
mislead 잘못 인도하다   exploit 이용하다   represent 대표하다
encompass 포함하다

근거

She was chosen to represent her country in the upcoming international conference, where she showcased her expertise in diplomacy and economics.

정답 ③

주요 어휘 정리
exploit 이용하다   encompass 포함하다
= take advantage of   = include
  utilize   involve
  harness   contain
  trade on   comprise
  avail oneself of
  capitalize on

164 밑줄 친 부분에 들어갈 말로 가장 적절한 것은?

> A: I think we're going to have a great time as roommates.
> B: Are you a morning person or a night person?
> A: I'm very flexible with sleeping times. _____
> B: I should be fine too unless you blast the music while I'm sleeping.
> A: Great! By the way, did you eat lunch yet?
> B: No. Is there a cafeteria in the building?
> A: Yeah. I'll show you.

① I think I'm a morning person.
② How do you like the music?
③ They have a strict rule about noise level.
④ Besides, a little noise never bothers me.

165 밑줄 친 부분에 들어갈 말로 가장 적절한 것은?

Emma Davies
Hey, Luke, did you know it's Karen's birthday tomorrow?
10:42

 Luke Hall
Really? I didn't realize. Are we doing something for her?
10:43

Emma Davies
Yes, I was thinking of getting a cake and some decorations. Want to help?
10:44

 Luke Hall
Absolutely. _____.
10:45

Emma Davies
I'll get the cake, then. Let's meet early tomorrow to set everything up.
10:46

 Luke Hall
Sounds like a plan. See you then!
10:47

① I'll buy a cake on my way there
② I haven't decided what to get for her
③ I'll take care of the decorations
④ I'm the last person to tell anybody

164

> A: 우리가 룸메이트로서 즐거운 시간을 보낼 수 있을 것 같네요.
> B: 아침형 인간이세요, 저녁형 인간이세요?
> A: 저는 자는 시간에 굉장히 유연해요. 게다가, 조금 시끄러운 것은 절대 신경 쓰지 않아요.
> B: 제가 자는 동안 당신이 음악을 크게 틀어대지만 않는다면, 저도 괜찮아요.
> A: 좋아요! 그런데 점심은 드셨나요?
> B: 아니요. 건물 안에 구내식당이 있나요?
> A: 네. 제가 안내해드릴게요.

① 전 아침형 인간인 것 같아요.
② 음악이 마음에 드세요?
③ 소음 수준에 대한 엄격한 규정이 있어요.

[어휘] flexible 유연한   cafeteria 구내식당   strict 엄격한
besides 게다가   bother 신경 쓰이게 하다

[정답] ④

165

Emma Davies 이봐, Luke, 내일 Karen 생일인 거 알았어? 10:42

Luke Hall 정말? 난 몰랐어. 우리가 그녀를 위해 뭔가를 할거야? 10:43

Emma Davies 그럼, 케이크와 장식품을 사려고 생각 중이었어. 도와줄 수 있어? 10:44

Luke Hall 물론이지. 장식품은 내가 책임질게. 10:45

Emma Davies 그러면 나는 케이크를 맡을게. 내일 일찍 만나서 모든 걸 준비하자. 10:46

Luke Hall 좋은 생각이야. 그때 봐! 10:47

① 거기로 가는 길에 케이크를 살게
② 그녀를 위해 무엇을 사야 할지 결정하지 못했어
④ 난 절대 아무에게도 말할 사람 아냐

[어휘] decoration 장식(품)   Sounds like a plan. 좋은 생각이야.
take care of ~을 책임지다
the last person to 절대 ~하지 않을 사람

[정답] ③

166 밑줄 친 부분에 들어갈 말로 가장 적절한 것은?

> After a long day of hiking, we were _____ and got ready to rest.

① sturdy ② weary
③ delightful ④ vigorous

167 밑줄 친 부분에 들어갈 말로 가장 적절한 것은?

> Despite the economic upheaval of a global pandemic, generous donors showed their _____ for people in need around the world.

① compassion ② profitability
③ contradiction ④ severance

168 밑줄 친 부분에 들어갈 말로 가장 적절한 것은?

> A: I had a wonderful time at dinner tonight.
> B: Me too! The food was excellent.
> A: So, shall we ask for the bill?
> B: Sure. Let's split it.
> A: I will treat you tonight.
> B: Are you sure? That's very kind of you.
> A: And _____.
> B: Right. We should take turns.

① you can get the tab the next
② you should make a right turn
③ I will go to the restaurant with you
④ I will buy you some food next week

166

[해석] 긴 하루의 하이킹 후에, 우리는 지쳤고 쉴 준비를 했다.

[어휘] get ready to ~할 준비를 하다　sturdy 튼튼한　weary 지친
delightful 정말 기분 좋은　vigorous 활발한

[근거]

> After a long day of hiking, we were weary and got ready to rest.

[정답] ②

[주요 어휘 정리]

sturdy 튼튼한	weary 지친
= strong	= tired
robust	exhausted
	worn-out
	fatigued

167

[해석] 세계적인 유행병으로 인한 경제적 격변에도 불구하고, 후한 기부자들은 전 세계의 도움이 필요한 사람들에 대한 그들의 연민을 보여줬다.

[어휘] upheaval 격변　pandemic 세계적 유행병
generous 후한　donor 기부자　compassion 연민
profitability 수익성　contradiction 모순　severance 단절

[근거]

> Despite the economic upheaval of a global pandemic, generous donors showed their compassion for people in need around the world.

[정답] ①

[주요 어휘 정리]
compassion 연민, 동정심
= sympathy
　mercy
　pity
　kindness

168

A: 오늘 저녁 식사는 정말 즐거웠어요.
B: 저도요! 음식이 훌륭했어요.
A: 그럼 계산서를 달라고 할까요?
B: 그러죠. 나눠서 냅시다.
A: 오늘 밤은 제가 한턱낼게요.
B: 정말요? 정말 고마워요.
A: 그리고 다음번에는 당신이 계산하면 되잖아요.
B: 그래요. 우리 번갈아 가면서 계산해요.

② 너는 우회전을 해야 해
③ 당신하고 그 식당에 갈게요
④ 다음 주에 음식을 살게요

[어휘] excellent 훌륭한　bill 계산서　split (몫을) 나누다　treat 한턱내다
take turns 번갈아가면서 하다　get the tab 계산하다

[정답] ①

DAY 17　143

169 밑줄 친 부분에 들어갈 말로 가장 적절한 것은?

> When falling short of chairs, they can't ask guests to offer their seats to others, so such sacrifice should be _____; it's not an obligation.

① voluntary ② compulsory
③ mandatory ④ instinctive

170 밑줄 친 부분에 들어갈 말로 가장 적절한 것은?

> The new policy initiatives are expected to _____ significant changes in how the company operates its sustainability programs, potentially reducing carbon emissions by 30% within the next fiscal year.

① cause ② cease
③ suppress ④ shield

169

해석 의자가 부족할 때, 그들이 손님에게 의자를 다른 사람에게 양보하라고 요구할 수 없으므로, 그런 희생은 자발적이어야 한다: 그것은 의무가 아니다.

어휘 fall short of ~이 부족하다   sacrifice 희생   obligation 의무
voluntary 자발적인   compulsory 의무적인
mandatory 의무적인   instinctive 본능적인

근거
> When falling short of chairs, they can't ask guests to offer their seats to others, so such sacrifice should be voluntary; it's not an obligation.

정답 ①

주요 어휘 정리
mandatory 의무적인
= compulsory
  obligatory
  required

170

해석 새로운 정책 계획들은 회사가 지속 가능성 프로그램을 운영하는 방식에 상당한 변화를 초래할 것으로 예상되며, 잠재적으로 다음 회계 연도 내에 탄소 배출량을 30% 감소시킬 것이다.

어휘 policy 정책   initiative 계획   significant 상당한
sustainability 지속 가능성   potentially 잠재적으로
carbon 탄소   emission 배출량   fiscal year 회계 연도
cause 초래하다   cease 중단하다   suppress 진압하다
shield 보호하다

근거
> The new policy initiatives are expected to cause significant changes in how the company operates its sustainability programs, potentially reducing carbon emissions by 30% within the next fiscal year.

정답 ①

주요 어휘 정리
cause 초래하다   cease 중단하다
= bring about   = stop
  lead to   end
  result in   discontinue
                             halt
suppress 진압하다   quit
= repress
  control
  quell
  put down
  keep down

DAY 17

171 밑줄 친 부분에 들어갈 말로 가장 적절한 것은?

> A: Are you hurt? You have a bruised eye. Did you get into a fight or something?
> B: My brother did it to me! I can't stand it any more. He's got to pay for it.
> A: _____
> B: Well, actually, I drove his car without his permission and crashed into another car.
> A: You really did so? No wonder why he hit you.
> B: But the damages are barely noticeable! It was just a fender bender!

① Do you think that doesn't make him a bad person?
② He wouldn't do such a thing without a good reason.
③ Who on earth did give you a permission to hit him?
④ I have heard what happened between you two.

172 밑줄 친 부분에 들어갈 말로 가장 적절한 것은?

Josh Kang
Hi Naomi, I'm here to give you an update on the project.
10:42

 Naomi Brown
Hi Josh, please go ahead.
10:43

Josh Kang
We've received the first draft from the design team. We plan to incorporate the feedback by tomorrow.
10:44

 Naomi Brown
Sounds good. _____ _____?
10:45

Josh Kang
The survey data has been collected and analysts is assessing how reliable the sample is.
10:46

 Naomi Brown
Got it. Please provide weekly updates on each part's progress.
10:47

Josh Kang
Will do. Thank you.
10:48

① Did you hire analysts under the procedure
② How is marketing research going
③ Can you give a progress report regularly
④ Is there anything I can help you with

171

A: 너 다쳤니? 눈이 멍들었네. 싸움에 휘말리거나 뭐 그런 거야?
B: 우리 형이 그랬어! 더는 못 참겠어. 형도 당해봐야 해.
A: 그가 정당한 이유 없이 그랬을 리가 없는데.
B: 음, 사실, 내가 형 차를 허락 없이 몰고 나갔다가 다른 차량과 충돌 했어.
A: 너가 정말 그랬어? 형이 왜 널 때렸는지 알 만하다.
B: 하지만 손상은 거의 눈에 띄지도 않아. 그건 단순히 접촉 사고였다고!

① 그렇다고 그가 나쁜 사람이 되는 것은 아니라고 생각해?
③ 대체 누가 너에게 그를 때려도 된다고 허락한 거야?
④ 너희 둘 사이에 무슨 일이 있었는지 들었어.

어휘 bruised 멍든   stand 참다   pay for (보복을) 당하다
permission 허락   crash into ~와 충돌하다   damage 손상
noticeable 눈에 띄는   fender bender 접촉 사고

정답 ②

172

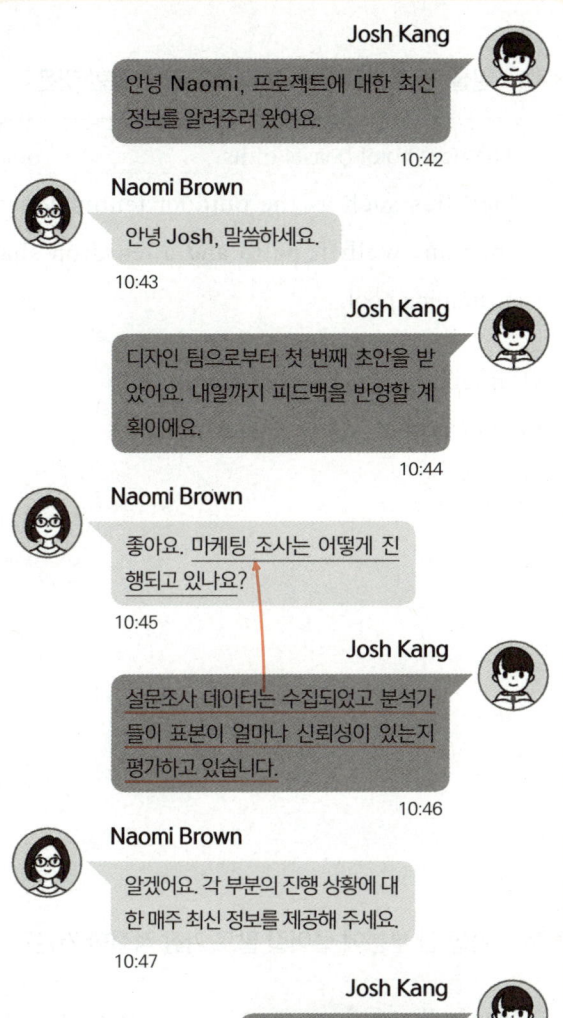

① 분석가들을 절차대로 고용했나요
③ 진행 보고를 정기적으로 해주시겠어요
④ 제가 도와드릴 만한 일이 있을까요

어휘 Go ahead. 말씀하세요.   draft 초안   incorporate 반영하다
survey 설문조사   analyst 분석가   assess 평가하다
reliable 신뢰성 있는   sample 표본   hire 채용하다
under the procedure 절차대로   regularly 정기적으로

정답 ②

173 밑줄 친 부분에 들어갈 말로 가장 적절한 것은?

The new hotel boasts of its _____ outdoor facilities such as the outdoor tennis courts, a spacious well-lit patio and a teardrop-shaped swimming pool.

① fragile ② surprised
③ impeccable ④ worthless

174 밑줄 친 부분에 들어갈 말로 가장 적절한 것은?

The bully tried to _____ the new student with aggressive behavior.

① coordinate ② negotiate
③ intimidate ④ assist

175 밑줄 친 부분에 들어갈 말로 가장 적절한 것은?

 Mia Barns
Where are you planning to hold your party this time?
10:42

 Bill Brison
I don't know. I used to hold the Christmas party at a fancy restaurant.
10:43

 Mia Barns
Yeah, that was fantastic.
10:44

 Bill Brison
But it always cost an arm and a leg.
10:45

 Mia Barns
You're absolutely right. _____
10:46

 Bill Brison
Great idea! That way, we can save money and everybody will admire my plants.
10:47

① Why don't you stick to a fancy restaurant?
② I can't go to the party because I hurt my leg.
③ How about holding a simple garden party?
④ It will be very hard to satisfy everyone.

173

해석 새 호텔은 야외 테니스 코트, 햇빛이 잘 드는 널찍한 테라스, 그리고 눈물방울 모양의 수영장과 같은 완벽한 야외 시설을 자랑한다.

어휘 boast 자랑하다 spacious 널찍한 fragile 약한
surprised 놀란(cf. surprising 놀라운) impeccable 완벽한
worthless 가치 없는

근거

> The new hotel boasts of its impeccable outdoor facilities such as the outdoor tennis courts, a spacious well-lit patio and a teardrop-shaped swimming pool.

정답 ③

주요 어휘 정리

fragile 약한, 깨지기 쉬운	impeccable 완벽한, 무결점의
= brittle	= faultless
breakable	flawless
feeble	immaculate
frail	unblemished
weak	perfect

174

해석 그 불량배는 공격적인 행동으로 신입생을 위협하려고 했다.

어휘 bully 불량배 aggressive 공격적인 behavior 행동
coordinate 조정하다 negotiate 협상하다
intimidate 위협하다 assist 돕다

근거

> The bully tried to intimidate the new student with aggressive behavior.

정답 ③

주요 어휘 정리

intimidate 위협하다	assist 돕다
= threaten	= help
browbeat	aid
menace	serve

175

① 고급 식당을 고수하는 게 어때?
② 나는 다리를 다쳐서 파티에 갈 수 없어.
④ 모두를 만족시키는 건 아주 어려울 거야.

어휘 fancy 고급의 cost an arm and a leg 엄청난 돈이 들다
absolutely 전적으로 stick to ~을 고수하다 satisfy 만족시키다

정답 ③

176 밑줄 친 부분에 들어갈 말로 가장 적절한 것은?

> Our team has clearly _____ the disappointment of last week's defeat, saying it was nothing more than a minor hiccup.

① dismissed ② contemplated
③ repaired ④ postpone

177 밑줄 친 부분에 들어갈 말로 가장 적절한 것은?

> Even after achieving something and rising in life, it is human nature to _____ for better things as well as higher places.

① advocate ② yearn
③ compensate ④ blame

178 밑줄 친 부분에 들어갈 말로 가장 적절한 것은?

> When a child is adopted, the new parents are required to _____ full legal responsibility for the child, that is, to formally take on all duties and obligations as the child's lawful guardians.

① reveal ② assume
③ delay ④ crave

176

[해석] 우리 팀은 지난주의 패배는 사소한 문제에 불과하다고 말하며 그것에 대한 실망감을 확실히 떨쳐 버렸다.

[어휘] disappointment 실망감 defeat 패배
nothing more than ~에 불과한 minor 사소한
hiccup 문제 dismiss 떨쳐 버리다 contemplate 심사숙고하다
repair 수리하다 postpone 미루다

[근거]
> Our team has clearly dismissed the disappointment of last week's defeat, saying it was nothing more than a minor hiccup.

[정답] ①

[주요 어휘 정리]

contemplate 심사숙고하다	postpone 미루다
= ponder	= defer
muse	delay
mull over	suspend
meditate	put off
deliberate	
ruminate	

177

[해석] 인생에서 무언가를 성취하고 인생에서 성공한 뒤에도, 더 높은 위치뿐만 아니라 더 좋은 것을 갈망하는 것은 인간의 본능이다.

[어휘] achieve 성취하다 rise 성공하다 nature 본능
advocate 지지하다 yearn 갈망하다 compensate 보상하다
blame 탓하다

[근거]
> Even after achieving something and rising in life, it is human nature to yearn for better things as well as higher places.

[정답] ②

[주요 어휘 정리]

yearn 갈망하다	blame 탓하다
= long	= criticize
crave	condemn
desire	denounce
want	
covet	

178

[해석] 아이가 입양될 경우, 새로운 부모는 그 아이에 대한 완전한 법적 책임을 맡는 것, 즉, 아이의 합법적인 보호자로서의 모든 의무와 책임을 공식적으로 인수하는 것이 요구된다.

[어휘] adopt 입양하다 legal 법적인 responsibility 책임 that is 즉
formally 공식적으로 take on ~을 인수하다 duty 의무
obligation 책임 lawful 합법적인 guardian 보호자
reveal 드러내다 assume 맡다 delay 연기하다 crave 갈망하다

[근거]
> When a child is adopted, the new parents are required to assume full legal responsibility for the child, that is, to formally take on all duties and obligations as the child's lawful guardians.

[정답] ②

179 밑줄 친 부분에 들어갈 말로 가장 적절한 것은?

> She is trying to be _____ to avoid a racial prejudice.

① picky ② political
③ impartial ④ biased

180 밑줄 친 부분에 들어갈 말로 가장 적절한 것은?

> A: Welcome to our cabin in the woods!
> B: Wow, what a beautiful place!
> A: I'm glad you like it. Let me know if you need anything.
> B: Thank you! Is there any place nearby where I can eat some food?
> A: Well, _____.
> B: That's more than enough.
> A: Great. I'll bring our menu.
> B: That sounds perfect.

① we can provide you with light snacks, though not a full meal
② you can enjoy snacks you've brought by the fireplace
③ many local food stores are around 300 meters from here
④ food is always the most important you should prepare

179

해석 그녀는 인종적 편견을 피하기 위해 공정하려고 노력하고 있다.

어휘 avoid 피하다 racial 인종적인 prejudice 편견 picky 까다로운 political 정치의 impartial 공정한 biased 편향된

근거

She is trying to be impartial to avoid a racial prejudice.

정답 ③

주요 어휘 정리
impartial 공정한
= fair
  just
  unbiased
  equitable

180

A: 저희의 숲속 오두막에 오신 것을 환영합니다!
B: 와, 정말 아름다운 곳이네요!
A: 마음에 드셨다니 다행이네요. 필요하신 게 있으시면 말씀해 주세요.
B: 감사합니다! 제가 음식을 먹을 수 있는 곳이 근처에 있을까요?
A: 음, 제대로 된 식사는 아니지만 가벼운 간식을 제공해드릴 수 있어요.
B: 그거면 충분하고도 남죠.
A: 좋습니다. 메뉴를 가져다드릴게요.
B: 그거 좋네요.

② 가지고 오신 간식을 벽난로 옆에서 즐기실 수 있어요
③ 많은 지역 식료품점이 여기서 300미터 정도의 거리에 있어요
④ 음식은 언제나 당신이 준비해야 하는 가장 중요한 거예요

어휘 cabin 오두막 full meal 제대로 된 식사 fireplace 벽난로 local 지역의

정답 ①

181 밑줄 친 부분에 들어갈 말로 가장 적절한 것은?

Customer: Hi there! I'm interested in hiring a party planner. 10:42

Party Planner: Hello! What type of event are you planning? 10:43

Customer: I'm throwing my daughter a graduation party for about 50 people. 10:44

Party Planner: Wonderful! Do you have a budget in mind for the event? 10:45

Customer: We're looking to stay around $5,000. 10:46

Party Planner: _____? 10:47

Customer: We're aiming for preferably a venue with outdoor space. 10:48

Party Planner: Understood. I'll create a package tailored to your preference. 10:49

① Do you have any specific decoration requirements
② Are there any particular preferences for food
③ Where would you like the party to take place
④ Do you have a specific atmosphere in mind

182 밑줄 친 부분에 들어갈 말로 가장 적절한 것은?

A: Hi, I'd like to withdraw $1,000 from my account, please.
B: I'm sorry, but withdrawing $1,000 would bring your balance below the minimum balance.
A: What happens if I lower the minimum required?
B: Lowering the minimum balance adversely affects your account's benefits and results in charges.
A: Hmm, I didn't realize that. In that case, _____.
B: That's a good idea. Then how much would you like to withdraw?
A: Just half of what I requested.

① What you've told me makes me want more money
② I want to hold off on withdrawal just in case
③ I would like to maintain the minimum balance
④ I had better close my account for a while

181

① 특정 장식 요구 사항이 있습니까
② 음식에 대한 특별한 선호 사항이 있습니까
④ 염두에 둔 특정 분위기가 있습니까

어휘 event 행사 throw a party 파티를 열다 graduation 졸업 budget 예산 in mind 염두에 둔 look to ~할 예정이다 aim 목표로 하다 preferably 가급적이면 venue 장소 tailored to ~에 맞춘 preference 선호 requirement 요구 사항 atmosphere 분위기

정답 ③

182

A: 안녕하세요, 제 계좌에서 1,000달러를 인출하고 싶습니다.
B: 죄송하지만, 1,000달러를 인출하시면 잔액이 최소 잔액 아래로 내려가게 됩니다.
A: 제가 최소 잔액을 낮추면 어떻게 되나요?
B: <u>최소 잔액을 낮추면 고객님의 계좌 혜택에 악영향을 주고 결과적으로 요금도 발생합니다.</u>
A: 음, 그건 몰랐어요. 그렇다면, <u>최소 잔액을 유지하고 싶어요.</u>
B: 좋은 생각이십니다. 그러면 얼마를 인출하시겠어요?
A: 요청한 액수의 절반만요.

① 당신 말을 듣고 보니 더 많은 돈을 원하게 되네요
② 만약을 위해서 인출을 보류하고 싶어요
④ 제 계좌를 당분간 닫아버리는 게 낫겠어요

어휘 withdraw 인출하다 account 계좌 balance 잔액 minimum 최소의 adversely affect 악영향을 주다 benefit 혜택 charge 요금 realize 깨닫다 hold off on ~을 보류하다 withdrawal 인출 just in case 만약을 위해서 maintain 유지하다 for a while 당분간

정답 ③

183 밑줄 친 부분에 들어갈 말로 가장 적절한 것은?

> Her _____ nature made her a great researcher, always eager to ask questions and seek out new information.

① passive   ② indifferent
③ reserved   ④ inquisitive

184 밑줄 친 부분에 들어갈 말로 가장 적절한 것은?

> The latest version of the software is _____ with older operating systems, which means that users with older computers can still enjoy its new features without any issues.

① compatible   ② dominant
③ incongruous   ④ abstract

185 밑줄 친 부분에 들어갈 말로 가장 적절한 것은?

> A: How's my dog doing? Any updates?
> B: He's stable but still under observation for a respiratory infection.
> A: I hope he gets better soon. _____?
> B: Just visit him and keep him calm. We'll update you if anything changes when you're not here.
> A: Got it. Thanks!

① Can I take him home now
② Is there anything I can do
③ Should I drug him regularly
④ Will he be hospitalized

183

해석 그녀의 호기심 많은 성격은 그녀를 훌륭한 연구자로 만들었고, 그녀는 항상 질문을 하고 새로운 정보를 찾기에 열심이었다.

어휘 nature 성격 eager 열심인 seek out 찾다 passive 수동적인 indifferent 무관심한 reserved 내성적인 inquisitive 호기심 많은

근거
> Her inquisitive nature made her a great researcher, always eager to ask questions and seek out new information.

정답 ④

주요 어휘 정리
reserved 내성적인, 말이 없는 ↔ outgoing 외향적인
= reticent   = extroverted
  uncommunicative   sociable

inquisitive 호기심 많은
= curious

184

해석 소프트웨어의 최신 버전은 오래된 운영 체제와 호환이 가능한데, 이는 오래된 컴퓨터를 사용하는 사용자가 아무 문제없이 새로운 기능들을 여전히 즐길 수 있다는 뜻이다.

어휘 latest 최신의 operating system 운영 체제 feature 기능 compatible 호환 가능한 dominant 우세한 incongruous 부조화한 abstract 추상적인

근거
> The latest version of the software is compatible with older operating systems, which means that users with older computers can still enjoy its new features without any issues.

정답 ①

주요 어휘 정리
compatible 호환 가능한   abstract 추상적인 ↔ concrete 구체적인
= consistent   = impalpable   = palpable
  harmonious   untouchable   touchable
  congruous   nonphysical   physical
  congruent   intangible   tangible

185

A: 제 강아지는 어떤가요? 새로운 소식이 있나요?
B: 안정적이지만 여전히 호흡기 감염병을 관찰받고 있는 중이에요.
A: 강아지가 빨리 나아지면 좋겠어요. 제가 할 수 있는 일이 있을까요?
B: 그냥 면회 오셔서 진정 상태를 유지시켜 주세요. 당신이 여기에 없을 때 변화가 있으면 알려드리겠습니다.
A: 알겠습니다. 고맙습니다.

① 지금 집으로 데려갈 수 있을까요
③ 제가 약을 규칙적으로 먹여야 하나요
④ 입원시켜야 할까요

어휘 update 새로운 소식; (최신 정보를) 알려주다 stable 안정적인 under observation 관찰받는 respiratory 호흡기의 infection 감염(병) get better (병이) 나아지다 drug 약을 먹이다 regularly 규칙적으로 hospitalize 입원시키다

정답 ②

186 밑줄 친 부분에 들어갈 말로 가장 적절한 것은?

Liz Mongomery: My house was robbed last night. 10:42

Theo Lincoln: Are you serious? Did you report to the police? 10:43

Liz Mongomery: I did, and it is under investigation. 10:44

Theo Lincoln: How did that happen? 10:45

Liz Mongomery: I think _____. 10:46

Theo Lincoln: You should have taken security seriously. 10:47

Liz Mongomery: You're right. I should be more careful from now on. 10:49

① the robber busted my window
② I know who did this
③ he set the door alarm
④ I forgot to lock the door

187 밑줄 친 부분에 들어갈 말로 가장 적절한 것은?

In her first Instagram post, the movie star would sing, dance, pose her way through the streets of New York, and _____ her glamorous outfit and unbothered attitude. Big crowds gathered wherever she showed up.

① conceal
② shrink
③ flatter
④ brag

186

① 강도가 창문을 부순 것
② 누가 했는지 아는 것
③ 그가 현관 경보 장치를 설치한 것

어휘 rob 강도질을 하다   investigation 수사   security 보안
bust 부수다   door alarm 현관 경보 장치

정답 ④

187

해석 그녀의 첫 번째 인스타그램 게시물에서 그 스타 영화배우는 노래하고 춤을 추고 포즈를 취하며 뉴욕 거리를 누비며 화려한 의상과 신경 쓰지 않는 태도를 뽐냈다. 그녀가 나타나는 곳마다 많은 군중이 모였다.

어휘 post 게시물
pose one's way through 포즈를 취하며 ~ 전역을 돌아다니다
glamorous 화려한   outfit 의상   unbothered 신경 쓰지 않는
show up 나타나다   conceal 감추다   shrink 수축시키다
flatter 우쭐하게 하다   brag 뽐내다

근거

> In her first Instagram post, the movie star would sing, dance, pose her way through the streets of New York, and brag her glamorous outfit and unbothered attitude. Big crowds gathered wherever she showed up.

정답 ④

주요 어휘 정리

conceal 숨기다
= hide
  veil

brag 자랑하다, 과시하다
= boast
  show off

flatter 아첨하다, 우쭐하게 하다
= make up to
  play up to
  butter up
  praise

DAY 19   159

188 밑줄 친 부분에 들어갈 말로 가장 적절한 것은?

> If asked to give any words of advice for young people as a grown-up, I'd like to tell them that they should invest their time and money more into things like knowledge, instead of only into buying _____ things such as fancy-looking bags or shoes.

① incisive ② perennial
③ tangible ④ abstract

189 밑줄 친 부분에 들어갈 말로 가장 적절한 것은?

> A: Hello, Dr. Evans. It's nice to finally meet you.
> B: Pleasure to see you, too.
> A: Can I have your autograph on this?
> B: Oh, it's my new book on quantum mechanics.
> A: Yes, I bought it as soon as it was published.
> B: I guess it could be too hard for lay readers to understand.
> A: _____.
> B: Oh, really? In that case, we can have an in-depth discussion on it.

① I don't know that much about the area
② I'm in the doctoral program in physics
③ You don't need to be that judgmental
④ You can have my book if you want

190 밑줄 친 부분에 들어갈 말로 가장 적절한 것은?

> These domestic skills are _____ from mother to daughter, through the generations. Often the lessons are learned by chance — as a daughter plays in the room while a mother sews or cooks.

① regressed ② eradicated
③ converted ④ inherited

188

해석 만일 내가 어른으로서 청년들에게 조언해 줄 것을 요청받으면, 나는 그들에게 멋져 보이는 가방이나 신발과 같은 유형의 것들만 사는 대신 그들의 시간과 돈을 지식과 같은 것에 더 투자하라고 말하고 싶다.

어휘 advice 조언 grown-up 어른 invest 투자하다
knowledge 지식 fancy-looking 멋져 보이는 incisive 예리한
perennial 지속되는 tangible 유형의, 실재하는
abstract 추상적인

근거

> If asked to give any words of advice for young people as a grown-up, I'd like to tell them that they should invest their time and money more into things like knowledge, instead of only into buying tangible things such as fancy-looking bags or shoes.

정답 ③

주요 어휘 정리

incisive 예리한	↔ dull 둔한
= keen	= blunt
sharp	

perennial 지속되는, 영원한	
= lasting	perpetual
everlasting	persistent
continual	incessant
forever	unceasing
permanent	ceaseless
	eternal

tangible	↔ intangible
유형의, 실재하는	무형의
= real	= abstract
actual	impalpable
concrete	
palpable	

189

A: 안녕하세요, Evans 박사님. 마침내 만나게 되어 반갑습니다.
B: 저도 만나서 기쁘군요.
A: 여기에 사인을 받을 수 있을까요?
B: 오, 양자 역학에 관한 제 신간이군요.
A: 네, 출간되자마자 구매했어요.
B: 전문 지식이 없는 독자들이 이해하기에는 너무 어려울 것 같은데요.
A: 저는 물리학 박사과정 프로그램에 재학 중이에요.
B: 오, 그래요? 그런 경우라면, 우리는 그것에 관해 깊이 있는 토론을 할 수 있겠네요.

① 저는 그 분야에 관해 그렇게 많이 아는 건 아니에요
③ 그렇게 비판적으로 구실 필요는 없잖아요
④ 원하시면 제 책을 가지셔도 됩니다

어휘 autograph 사인 quantum mechanics 양자 역학
lay 전문 지식이 없는 in-depth 깊이 있는 area 분야
doctoral 박사과정의 physics 물리학 judgmental 비판적인

정답 ②

190

해석 이러한 가정 기술은 어머니에서 딸로 세대를 통해 물려진다. 어머니가 바느질을 하거나 요리를 하는 동안 딸이 방에서 노는 것 같이 교육은 종종 우연히 일어난다.

어휘 domestic 가정의 generation 세대 by chance 우연히
sew 바느질하다 regress 퇴보하다 eradicate 근절하다
convert 전환하다 inherit 물려받다

근거

> These domestic skills are inherited from mother to daughter, through the generations. Often the lessons are learned by chance — as a daughter plays in the room while a mother sews or cooks.

정답 ④

주요 어휘 정리
eradicate 근절하다, 뿌리째 뽑다
= remove
  eliminate
  exterminate
  get rid of
  wipe out
  sweep out
  weed out
  root out

191 밑줄 친 부분에 들어갈 말로 가장 적절한 것은?

> His conscience troubled him until he decided to _____ his guilt to the authorities.

① confess ② conceal
③ embrace ④ tackle

193 밑줄 친 부분에 들어갈 말로 가장 적절한 것은?

> Despite facing challenges, their friendship remained _____ over the years.

① timid ② tentative
③ variable ④ constant

192 밑줄 친 부분에 들어갈 말로 가장 적절한 것은?

> A: Wow, this spaghetti is amazing!
> B: I'm glad you like it. I thought I'd experiment a bit with the sauce. I'm glad it turned out well.
> A: _____?
> B: Sure! There's plenty left. Help yourself. How was your day?
> A: Thanks! My day was busy, but now that I'm eating this delicious meal, I feel much better.
> B: I'm glad to hear that! Let me know if you need anything else.

① How much pasta did you make at once
② Would you have sauce left for later
③ I skipped lunch, so can I have some more
④ Can I help you with the dishes after dinner

191

[해석] 그의 양심은 그가 당국에 죄를 자백할 때까지 그를 괴롭혔다.

[어휘] conscience 양심 trouble 괴롭히다 guilt 죄
authorities (pl.) 당국 confess 자백하다 conceal 숨기다
embrace 받아들이다 tackle (문제, 일 등과) 씨름하다

[근거]

> His conscience troubled him until he decided to confess his guilt to the authorities.

[정답] ①

[주요 어휘 정리]

confess 자백하다	conceal 숨기다
= admit (to)	= hide
	veil

192

A: 와, 이 스파게티 정말 끝내줘요!
B: 좋아하시니 다행이네요. 소스를 조금 실험해 볼까 했거든요. 잘 나와서 다행이네요.
A: 제가 점심을 걸렀는데, 좀 더 먹어도 되나요?
B: 물론이죠! 많이 남았어요. 많이 드세요. 오늘 하루는 어떠셨나요?
A: 고마워요! 오늘 하루는 바빴는데 이렇게 맛있는 걸 먹으니 기분이 훨씬 좋아졌어요.
B: 다행이네요! 더 필요한 거 있으시면 말씀해주세요.

① 파스타를 한 번에 얼마나 많이 만드셨나요
② 나중을 위해서 소스를 남겨두시겠어요
④ 저녁 식사 후에 설거지를 도와드릴까요

[어휘] experiment with ~을 실험하다 turn out (결과가) 나오다
Help yourself. 많이 드세요. now that ~하니까 at once 한 번에
skip 거르다 help with the dishes 설거지를 돕다

[정답] ③

193

[해석] 어려움에 직면했지만, 그들의 우정은 수년간 계속 변함없었다.

[어휘] face 직면하다 challenge 어려움 timid 소심한
tentative 잠정적인 variable 변하는 constant 변함없는

[근거]

> Despite facing challenges, their friendship remained constant over the years.

[정답] ④

[주요 어휘 정리]

timid 소심한	constant 변함없는
= shy	= incessant
trepid	ceaseless
cowardly	permanent
	perpetual
	perennial

194 밑줄 친 부분에 들어갈 말로 가장 적절한 것은?

> If the recent economic recession continues unabated, the number of unemployed people will _____ to uncontrollable levels, which in turn, will lead to more serious economic breakdown.

① dwindle ② soar
③ persist ④ ameliorate

195 밑줄 친 부분에 들어갈 말로 가장 적절한 것은?

Ashley Parker
How did the interview with Ms. Taylor go?
10:42

Ben Hogan
It was really good. She was smart and well-prepared.
10:43

Ashley Parker
Glad to hear that! How was her response to the technical topics?
10:44

Ben Hogan
She explained everything clearly and didn't stumble at all.
10:45

Ashley Parker
Sounds like she could be a good fit for the team.
10:46

Ben Hogan
Absolutely. She was genuinely interested in our company.
10:47

Ashley Parker
That's great. _____ _____?
10:48

Ben Hogan
I'll write an evaluation form and HR will assess it and make a decision.
10:49

① What's the process of employee termination
② How can I streamline the hiring process
③ Who was in charge of the interview
④ What's gonna happen at the next stage

194

해석 만일 최근의 경제 불황이 수그러들지 않고 지속되면, 실업자의 수는 통제할 수 없는 수준까지 치솟을 것이고, 이는 결국 더 심각한 경제 붕괴를 초래할 것이다.

어휘 recession 불황   unabated 수그러들지 않는
uncontrollable 통제할 수 없는   in turn 결국   breakdown 붕괴
dwindle 줄어들다   soar 치솟다   persist 지속하다
ameliorate 개선되다

근거

> If the recent economic recession continues unabated, the number of unemployed people will soar to uncontrollable levels, which in turn, will lead to more serious economic breakdown.

정답 ②

주요 어휘 정리

dwindle 줄어들다   soar 치솟다
= reduce   = rise
  decline   surge
  decrease   skyrocket
  diminish   proliferate

195

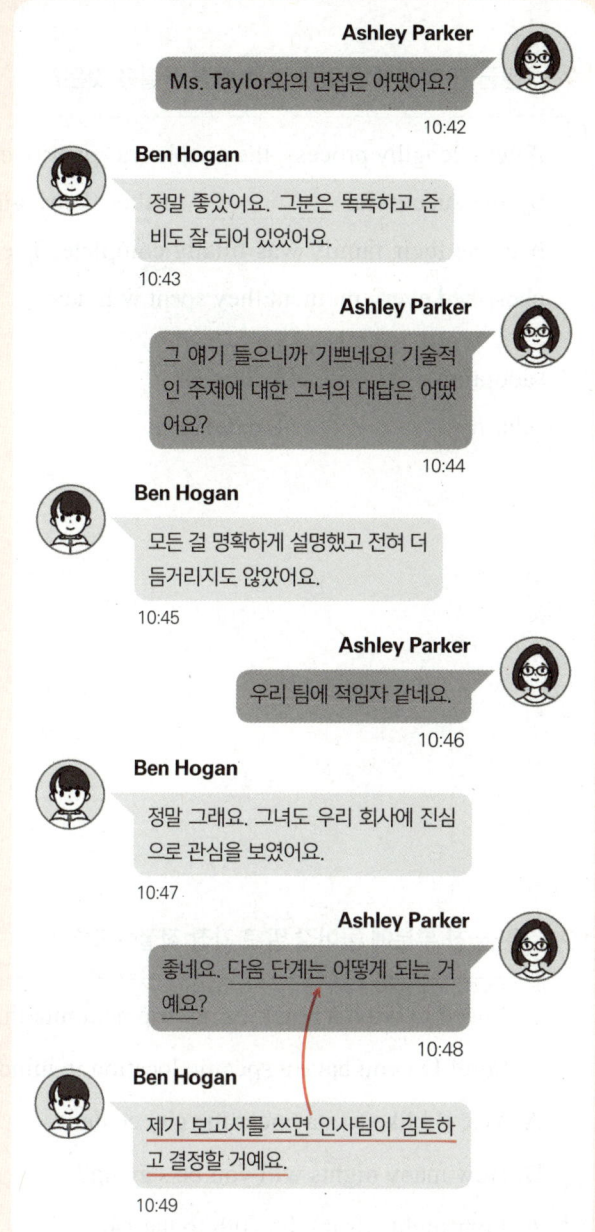

① 직원 해고 절차는 어떻게 되나요
② 채용 과정을 간소화하려면 어떻게 해야 되나요
③ 면접은 누가 맡았나요

어휘 well-prepared 준비가 잘 된   response 대답
stumble 더듬거리다   good fit 적임자   genuinely 진심으로
evaluation 평가   HR (human resources) 인사팀
assess 평가하다   process 절차   termination 해고
streamline 간소화하다   hire 채용하다   be in charge of ~을 맡다

정답 ④

196 밑줄 친 부분에 들어갈 말로 가장 적절한 것은?

After a lengthy process, the couple was overjoyed by the successful _____ of their baby girl because their family was finally complete. They cherished every moment they spent with her.

① adoption ② illusion
③ charity ④ extension

197 밑줄 친 부분에 들어갈 말로 가장 적절한 것은?

A: I need to book a hotel for my trip next month.
B: Sure! Do you have a specific location in mind?
A: Yes, I'd like to stay near the city center.
B: How many nights will you be staying?
A: Four nights, from the 10th to the 14th.
B: Okay, _____.
A: Sounds a bit pricey, but waking up to that kind of scenery might be worth it.

① there's no availability for four nights in that area.
② would you like us to wake you up in the morning?
③ there's a river-view room available for $150 per night.
④ do you want the pricey one or the cheaper option?

198 밑줄 친 부분에 들어갈 말로 가장 적절한 것은?

Hannah Baker
Andrew, did you choose a topic for the English essay?
10:42

Andrew Scott
I did.
10:43

Hannah Baker
Have you started writing it?
10:44

Andrew Scott
Not yet. I usually have a hard time making logical arguments for my essays. Do you have any suggestions?
10:45

Hannah Baker
Well, I read a lot of newspaper articles. If you read persuasive articles like editorials, you can see how the arguments are developed.
10:46

Andrew Scott
That makes sense to me. Maybe I should give it a try.
10:47

Hannah Baker
_____.
10:48

Andrew Scott
Thank you. That'll be very helpful for me to start reading editorials.
10:49

① Not all information written on articles is true
② I will send you links to the relevant articles
③ You had better find out references for yourself
④ It wouldn't hurt you to write in your own words

196

[해석] 긴 과정 끝에, 그 부부는 마침내 그들의 가족이 완성되었기 때문에 여자 아기를 성공적으로 입양한 것에 매우 기뻐했다. 그들은 그녀와 함께 보내는 모든 순간을 소중히 여겼다.

[어휘] lengthy 긴 overjoyed 매우 기뻐하는 complete 완성된
cherish 소중히 여기다 adoption 입양 illusion 착각
charity 자선 extension 확대

[근거]
> After a lengthy process, the couple was overjoyed by the successful <u>adoption</u> of their baby girl because <u>their family was finally complete</u>. They cherished every moment they spent with her.

[정답] ①

[주요 어휘 정리]
illusion 착각, 오해
= myth
  misunderstanding
  delusion
  misconception

197

> A: 다음 달 여행을 위해 호텔을 예약해야 해요.
> B: 네! 생각하고 계신 특정 위치가 있으신가요?
> A: 네, 도심부 근처에 머물고 싶어요.
> B: 몇 박을 머무실 건가요?
> A: 4박이요, 10일부터 14일까지요.
> B: 알겠습니다, 강 전망 객실을 하룻밤에 150달러로 이용할 수 있습니다.
> A: 가격이 좀 비싸긴 하지만, 그런 풍경을 보며 일어나는 건 그럴 만한 가치가 있을 것 같군요.

① 그 지역에는 나흘 동안 예약 가능한 방이 없습니다.
② 아침에 깨워드릴까요?
④ 비싼 쪽을 원하세요, 아니면 더 저렴한 걸 원하세요?

[어휘] book 예약하다 have ~ in mind ~을 생각하다 specific 특정한
location 위치 city center 도심부 pricey 비싼 scenery 경치

[정답] ③

198

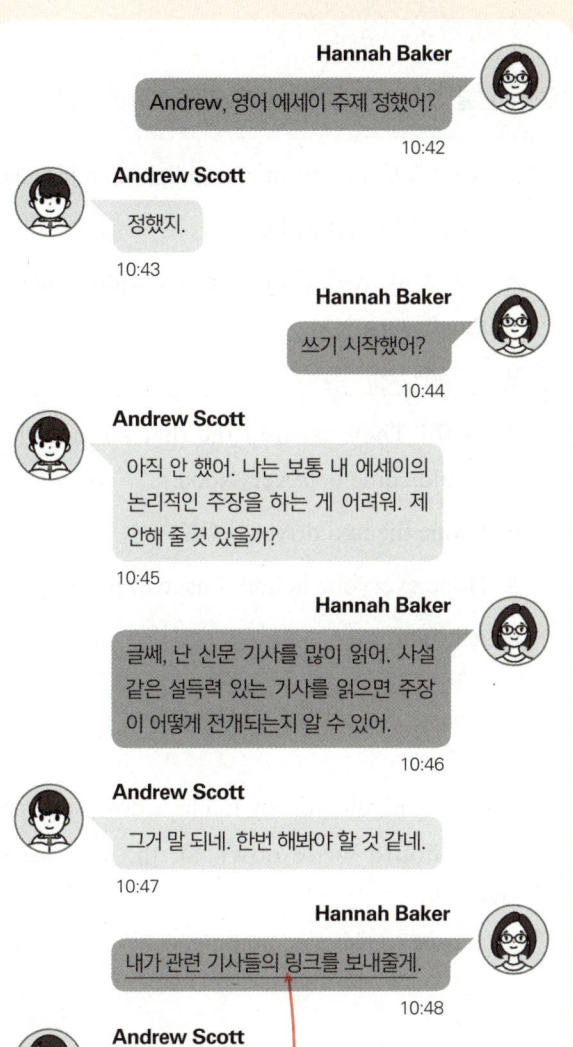

① 기사에 쓰인 모든 정보가 사실인 건 아니야
③ 네가 스스로 참고 자료를 찾는 게 좋아
④ 너만의 표현으로 글을 써서 해 될 건 없어

[어휘] have a hard time -ing ~하는 것이 어렵다 argument 주장
suggestion 제안 article 기사 persuasive 설득력 있는
editorial 사설 develop 전개하다 make sense 말이 되다
give it a try 한번 해보다 relevant 관련이 있는
reference 참고 자료 in one's own words ~만의 표현으로

[정답] ②

199 밑줄 친 부분에 들어갈 말로 가장 적절한 것은?

> A: Hey! A truck just ran a red light and hit a taxi!
> B: Oh no! Is anyone hurt?
> A: I was so freaked out that I couldn't check on the drivers.
> B: _____
> A: Yeah! They assured me that an ambulance would come here very soon.
> B: I hope the taxi driver is OK.
> A: Hope everyone is fine. I have to hang up now.
> B: All right, bye.

① At least, you called 911 and had them get help, right?
② Oh my god, did you try to chase down the truck?
③ You should write down all the details of the accident.
④ You used to drive an ambulance too, didn't you?

200 밑줄 친 부분에 들어갈 말로 가장 적절한 것은?

Mark Allen
Jenny, I'm afraid I cannot make it to our book club today. So, will you and David meet without me?
10:42

Jenny Campbell
Well... I have to miss it, too. I'm not feeling well.
10:43

Mark Allen
Oh no, I'm sorry to hear that. I hope it's nothing serious.
10:43

Jenny Campbell
Thanks. I just need some rest.
10:45

Mark Allen
I hope you feel better soon. Anyway, it seems we cannot meet today.
10:46

Jenny Campbell
_____
10:48

Mark Allen
Good idea. I'll text him now and see if tomorrow works.
10:48

① Why don't you put off visiting the doctor?
② Let's ask David if we can reschedule.
③ How about inviting David to our club?
④ We should find a place for today's meeting.

199

> A: 야! 어떤 트럭이 방금 빨간불을 무시하고 지나가서 택시를 들이받았어!
> B: 아 안 돼! 다친 사람은 없니?
> A: 내가 너무 놀라서 운전자들이 괜찮은지 살펴보지 못했어.
> B: 적어도, 911에 전화해서 그들이 도움을 받게 한 거지, 그렇지?
> A: 응! 그들은 구급차가 이리로 곧 올 거라고 장담했어.
> B: 택시 기사님이 괜찮으시길 바라.
> A: 모두들 괜찮으시길. 이제 전화 끊어야 해.
> B: 알았어, 안녕.

② 세상에, 그 트럭을 추적하려고 해봤니?
③ 너는 그 사고의 모든 세부 사항을 적어야만 해.
④ 너도 구급차를 운전했었잖아, 맞지?

어휘 freak out ~을 놀라게 하다   check on (이상이 없는지) 살펴보다
assure 장담하다   hang up 전화를 끊다
chase down ~을 추적하다

정답 ①

200

① 병원 방문을 미루는 게 어때?
③ David를 우리 모임에 초대하는 거 어때?
④ 오늘 모임을 위한 장소를 찾아야 해.

어휘 make it (모임에) 가다   miss 빠지다   serious 심각한
text 문자를 보내다   put off ~을 미루다
reschedule 일정을 다시 잡다   invite 초대하다

정답 ②

DAY 20 169

MEMO

MEMO

MEMO

MEMO

MEMO

MEMO

MEMO